My Book

This book belongs to

Cover Design by :
Gowri Vemuri

First Edition :
July , 2024

Author :
Gowri Vemuri

Edited by :
Ritvik Pothapragada

Questions: mathknots.help@gmail.com

NOTE : CCSSO or NCTM or VDOE is neither affiliated nor sponsors or endorses this product.

Dedication

This book is dedicated to:
My Mom, who is my best critic, guide and supporter.
To what I am today, and what I am going to become tomorrow,
is all because of your blessings, unconditional affection and support.

This book is dedicated to the
strongest women of my life ,
my dearest mom
and
to all those moms in this universe.

G.V.

Grade 7
Test 1

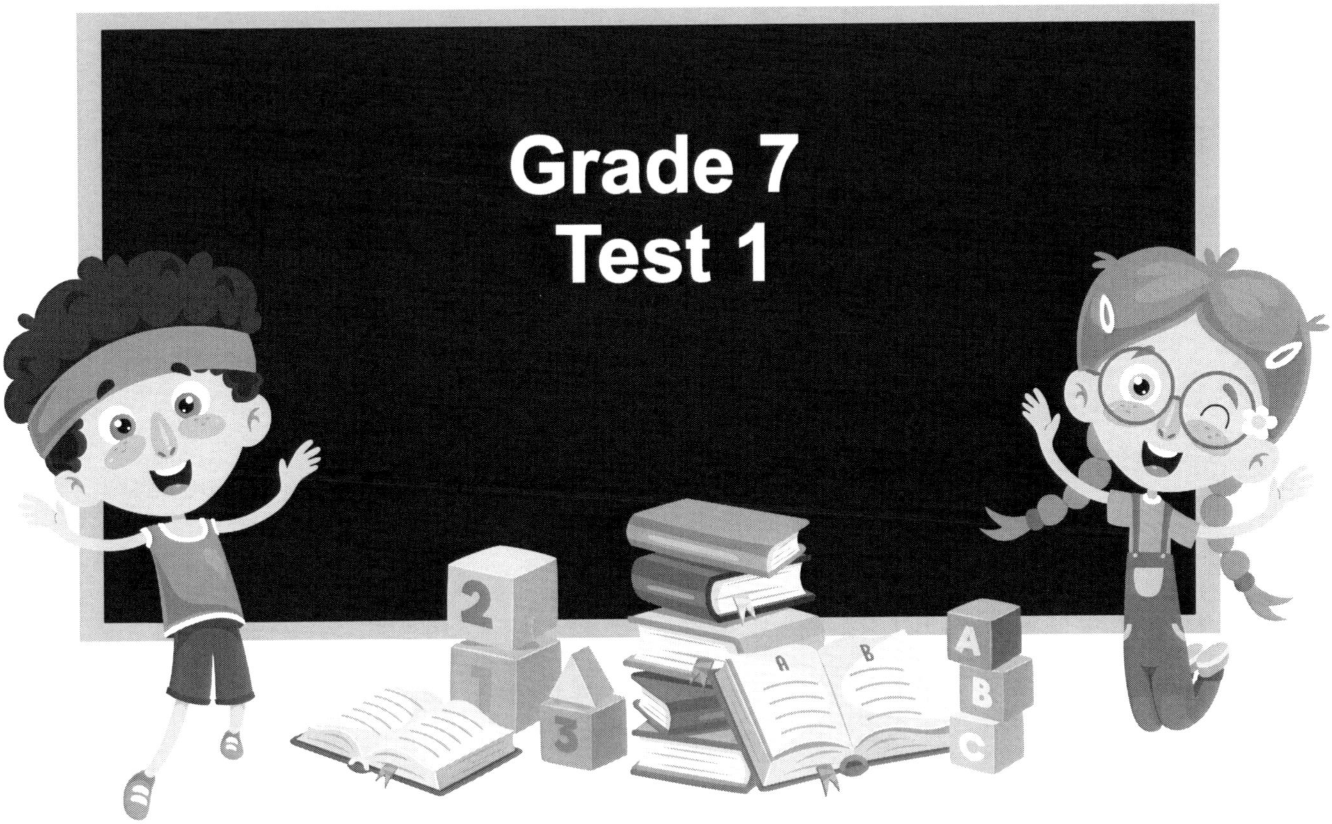

1) Simplify the below

$$\left| \frac{((-43) - (-1))}{7} \right|$$

(A) -7 (B) 19

(C) 6 (D) 20

2) Express the below number in scientific notation

990000

(A) 9.9×10^{-5} (B) 9.9×10^{-6}

(C) 9.9×10^{5} (D) 9.9×10^{6}

3) A rectangle is 25 in tall and 35 in wide. If it is reduced to a height of 5 in, then how wide will it be ?

(A) 25 in (B) 175 in

(C) 10 in (D) 7 in

4) Find the volume of the cylinder with a radius of 5 cm and a height of 5 cm.

(A) 329.9 cm^3 (B) 280.4 cm^3

(C) 140.2 cm^3 (D) 392.7 cm^3

5) Find the area of the enclosure.

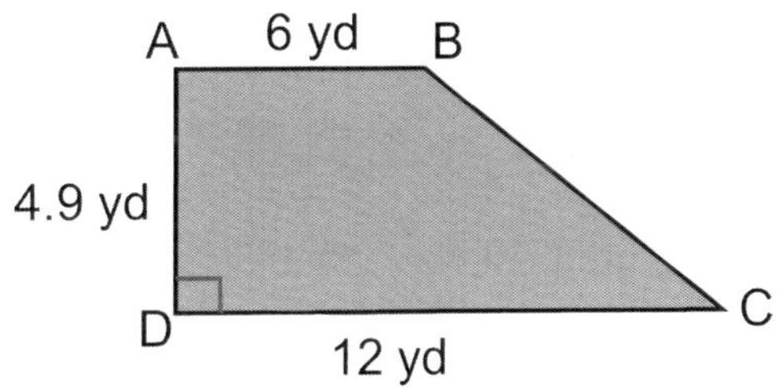

(A) 50.2 yd^2 (B) 22.1 yd^2

(C) 88.2 yd^2 (D) 44.1 yd^2

6) Find the total surface area of the given three dimensional shape.

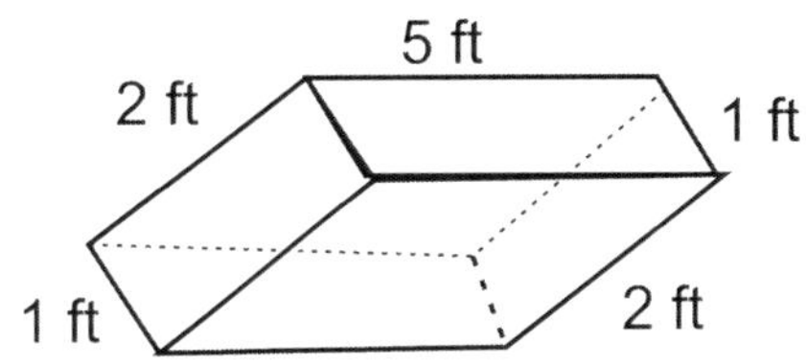

(A) 71 ft^2 (B) 34 ft^2

(C) 35.5 ft^2 (D) 39.4 ft^2

7) In how many ways the following task can be done ? A team of 6 basketball players need to choose a captain and co-captain.

(A) 30　　(B) 36

(C) 32　　(D) 26

8) Find the median for the given below data.
21 , 17 , 18 , 22 , 18 , 14 , 17 , 14 , 17 , 18 , 15

(A) 18　　(B) 17

(C) 14　　(D) 22

9) Find the mean age from the following data.

Age	Frequency
12	1
13	2
14	2
15	3
16	2
18	4
19	3
20	1
21	1
22	1
23	1

(A) 15.5

(B) 16.75

(C) 16.9

(D) 17.05

10) Simplify

$$-23 = -17 - v$$

(A) -6　　(B) -40

(C) $1\frac{6}{17}$　　(D) 6

11) Which of the below options describes

$$22g + 7 < 2 \text{ ?}$$

(A) Equation　　(B) Expression

(C) Inequality　　(D) Less than

12) Cathy spent $64 to buy a big box of snack bars. If each box cost $8, how many boxes did she buy ?

(A) 8　　(B) 7

(C) 10　　(D) 9

13) Jason spent $4.64 for a sandwich at lunch today. She now has $21.20. How much money did she had originally ?

(A) $25.84　　(B) $22.74

(C) $30.48　　(D) $16.56

14) Write an equation showing the relation between x & y.

x	y
1	5
2	6
5	9
10	14

(A) $y = 3x$

(B) $y = x + 4$

(C) $y = x - 4$

(D) $y = 5x$

15) The table below shows Math test scores of Grade 6 student

75 , 62 , 70 , 60 , 55

The teacher missed to add a student score. If the median and mode of the data is same. What is the missing score ?

(A) 62 (B) 55

(C) 75 (D) 60

16) Jack purchased a video game, originally priced at $52.50. He has a coupon for 57% discount. How much did Jack paid to the store for the game ?

(A) $23.85 (B) $25.8

(C) $22.58 (D) $22.90

17) Mia enlarged the size of a triangle to a base of 6 cm which originally “ had a base of 2 cm and a height of 4 cm. What is the height of the enlarged figure ?

(A) 12 cm (B) 15 cm

(C) 14 cm (D) 18 cm

18) The mass of an orchid seed is approximately 0.0000035 gram. Written in scientific notation, that mass is equivalent to 3.5×10^n. What is the value of <u>n</u> ?

(A) -8 (B) -6

(C) -7 (D) -5

19) Which of the below is less than 840% ?

(A) $8\frac{2}{5}$ (B) $\frac{21}{250}$

(C) 840 (D) $8\frac{1}{2}$

20) Rhombus ABCD and EFGH are congruent. Then what is the ratio of length $\overline{AD}$ to length $\overline{EH}$?

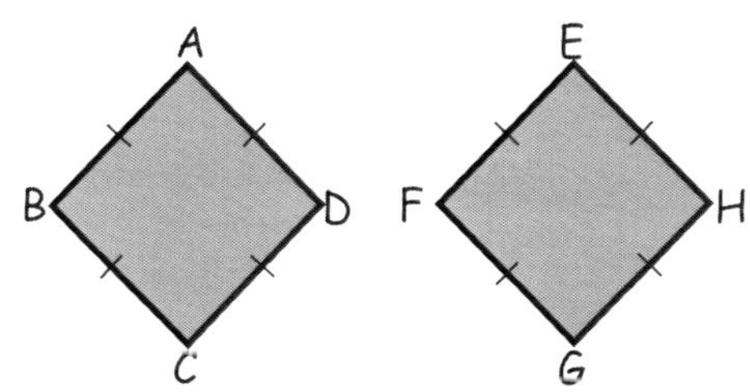

(A) 1 : 4 (B) 2 : 1

(C) 2 : 3 (D) 1 : 1

21) Find the value of x from the below triangles.

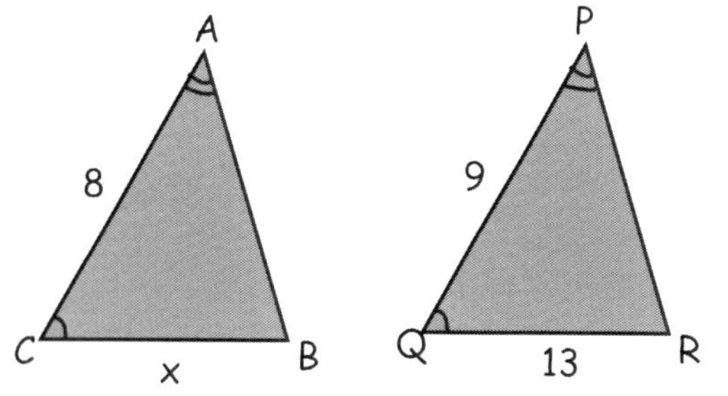

(A) $\frac{8}{x} = \frac{9}{13}$ (B) $\frac{x}{8} = \frac{9}{13}$

(C) $\frac{8}{x} = \frac{13}{9}$ (D) $8x = (13)(8)$

22) The temperature starts decreasing at a steady rate of -4° F per hour. How much will the temperature have dropped by the end of 10 hours ?

(A) -40° F (B) -6° F

(C) 14° F (D) 40° F

23) The average car sales at zoom cars across various days are plotted as the box and whisker plot.

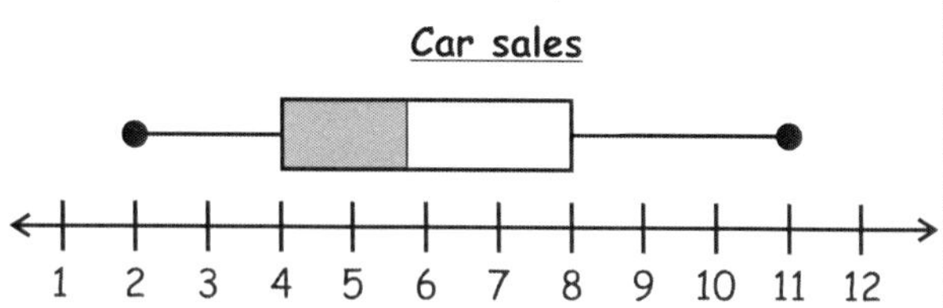

Find the range of the test scores based on the above data

(A) 5 (B) 7

(C) 10 (D) 9

24) Four identical poker chips - one red chip, one blue chip, one yellow chip, and one white chip - are placed in a paper bag. If you randomly draw two of the four chips out of the paper bag, what is the probability that you will draw the red and blue chips ?

(A) $\frac{1}{8}$ (B) $\frac{1}{6}$

(C) $\frac{1}{4}$ (D) $\frac{1}{3}$

25) A local ice cream store donates 2% of its sales of every Sunday to a local charity. Based on the information given

(A) Total sales amount of last Friday was \$1200 and donated \$24

(B) Total sales amount of last Friday was \$1100 and donated \$24

(C) Total sales amount of last Friday was \$120 and donated \$24

(D) Total sales amount of last Friday was \$24 and donated \$1200

Answers the questions 26-30 based on the data given below

Years	Classes									
	VI		VII		VIII		IX		X	
	A	F	A	F	A	F	A	F	A	F
2012	75	13	77	08	85	11	74	08	68	08
2013	67	17	80	09	83	06	79	06	69	15
2014	65	08	72	15	79	09	70	07	75	14
2015	69	06	66	11	77	12	71	04	84	09
2016	73	11	67	10	72	10	74	10	83	11
2017	72	12	76	07	84	05	80	05	72	05
2018	70	07	80	08	77	03	81	09	85	08

26) What is the number of passed students for all the classes together, in the Year 2018 ?

(A) 305 (B) 420

(C) 358 (D) 550

27) Find the average number of failed students from grade 8 for the given years.

(A) 8 (B) 9

(C) 7 (D) 11

28) Find the ratio of the total number of passed students to total number of failed students in the year 2015.

(A) 90:11 (B) 367:42

(C) 42:325 (D) 35:233

29) Find the total percentage of passed students of grade 9 from all the years together. (Round to 2 decimals)

(A) 91.88 (B) 74.92

(C) 85.95 (D) 91.52

30) Which of the below grade has the minimum number of passed students over the years ?

(A) Grade 8 (B) Grade 9

(C) Grade 7 (D) Grade 6

31) David purchased a game for $13.50. Find the selling price with a 5% tax added to it

(A) $14.18 (B) $15.52

(C) $16.20 (D) $12.82

32) Solve the below inequality

$$2 \geq \frac{x}{5} - 1$$

A) $x \leq -55$ B) $x \geq -26$

C) $x \leq 15$ D) $x \geq -55$

33) Simplify the below expression

$8.1(2m - 4.43) + 0.4$

A) $7.3 + 55.25m$

B) $-17.92 + 54.75m$

C) $-30.28 + 3.3m$

D) $16.2m - 35.483$

34) Evaluate the below using the values given

$$\left(\frac{c}{2}\right)^3 + ca$$

Given : $a = -8$, and $c = -2$

A) 14 B) 1

C) 0 D) 15

35) Find the surface area of the below figure

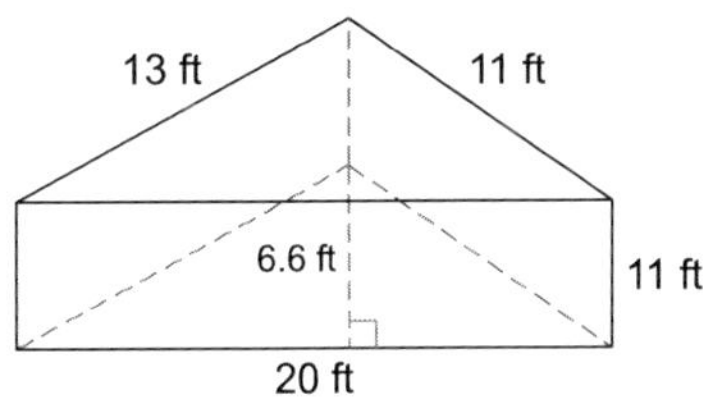

A) 677.6 ft² B) 616 ft²

C) 1612.6 ft² D) 806.3 ft²

36) Solve the below inequality

$171 \geq -9(x-8)$

A) $x \leq -2$ B) $x \geq -11$

C) $x \geq 11$ D) $x \geq -2$

37) Evaluate the below using the values given

$h-(8j^2+17)$

Given : $h=-17$, and $j=4$

A) −169 B) −162

C) −146 D) −161

38) Simplify the below figure

$-6(x+8)+15(3+x)$

A) $80x+302$ B) $286+246x$

C) $80x+317$ D) $9x-3$

39) Simplify the below figure

$-\frac{26}{7}+\frac{7}{2}\left(\frac{4}{3}a-\frac{7}{9}\right)$

A) $-\frac{9}{4}+\frac{7}{4}a$

B) $-\frac{811}{126}+\frac{53}{9}a$

C) $-\frac{811}{126}+\frac{14}{3}a$

D) $-\frac{577}{126}+\frac{53}{9}a$

40) Solve the below equation

$$-379 = 17 - 12k$$

A) 33 B) 10

C) −12 D) 25

41) A rectangular prism measuring 12 in and 8 in along the base and 16 in tall. Find the volume

A) 1002.2 in² B) 1138.9 in²

C) 832 in² D) 973.4 in²

42) Solve the below equation

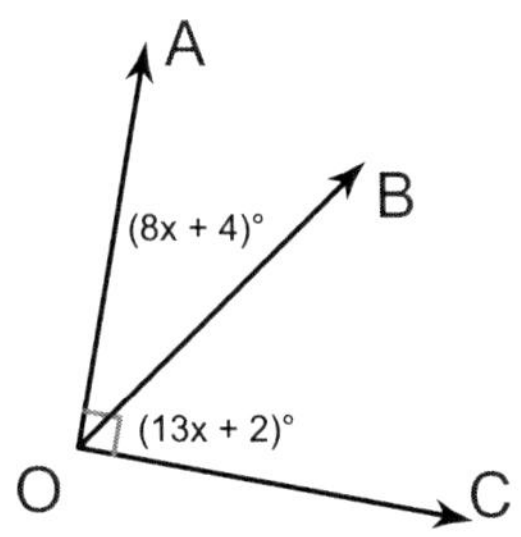

A) 4 B) -20

C) -9 D) -21

43) A square prism measuring 14 ft along each edge of the base and 10 ft tall. Find the volume.

A) 1087.8 ft³ B) 946.4 ft³

C) 1960 ft³ D) 980 ft³

44) Find the volume of x

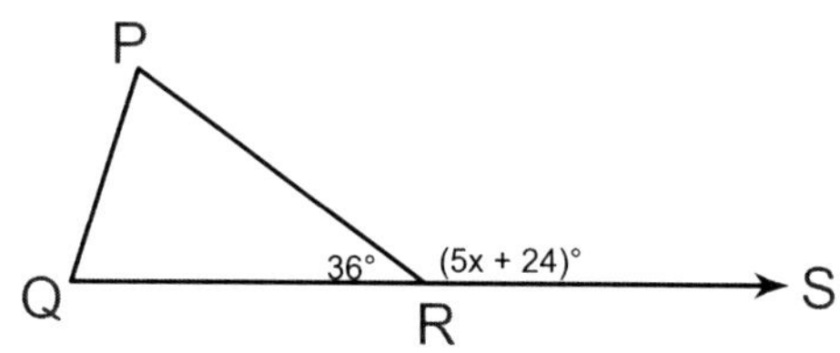

A) 24 B) 61

C) 41 D) 40

45) Find the volume of x

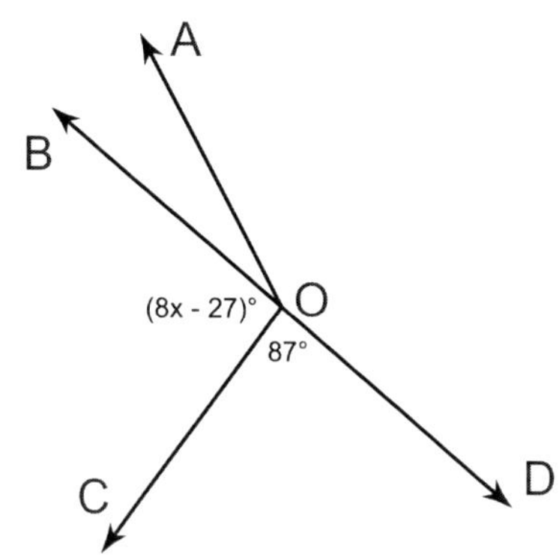

A) 12 B) 22

C) 15 D) 17

46) Four pineapples costs \$6.76. What is the price of one pineapple?

47) Mrs G bought 25 books for \$20. Find the unit rate of a book

48) The money used in China is called the Yuan. The exchange rate is \$1 to 7.7 Yuan. Find how many dollars you would receive if you exchanged 9.2 Yuan.

49) Find the distance between Rockville and Gainesville if they are 10 in apart on a map with a scale of 1 in : 19 mi.

50) Which two measures are equal in the two data sets provided below

Birth rate in Virginia

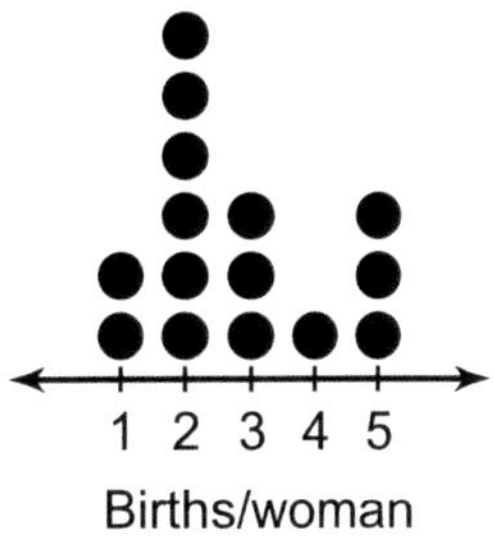

Birth rate in Texas

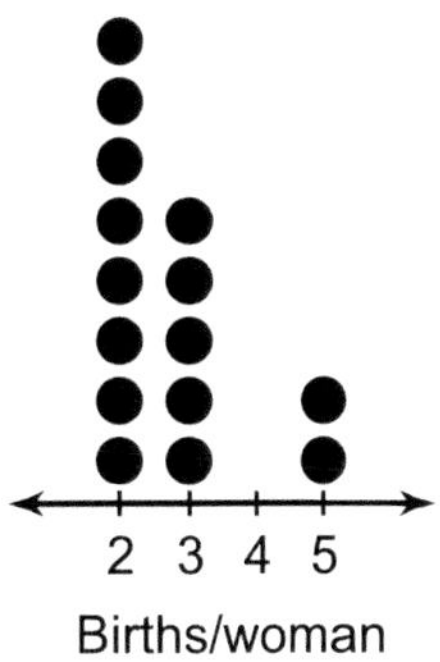

(A) Mean value is same in both data sets

(B) Mean and mode values are same

(C) Mode and median are same

(D) Median and mean are same

51) Compare the data measures of the below data sets

Shoe size of tenth grade students

8.5 8 8 9 9.5 8.5 10
6 8 6 12 8 8 8
4 9

Shoe size of eighth grade students

8 9 7 8 7.5 8.5 9
7 6.5 5 7 6.5 8.5 11
6.5 7

(A) Median value of eighth grade students is 0.75 less than tenth grade students

(B) Mode value is same for both

(C) Median value of eighth grade students is 0.75 greater than tenth grade students

(D) Mean value of eighth grade students is 0.65 greater than tenth grade students

52) A bag contains 3 pennies, 2 nickels and 4 dimes. If you select 3 coins without replacing them what is the probability that you will pick 3 pennies in a row?

53) A rectangular room is 14 ft by 15 ft has a semi circular morning room attached whose diameter is 12 ft. Find the total area of the room and the sitting area.

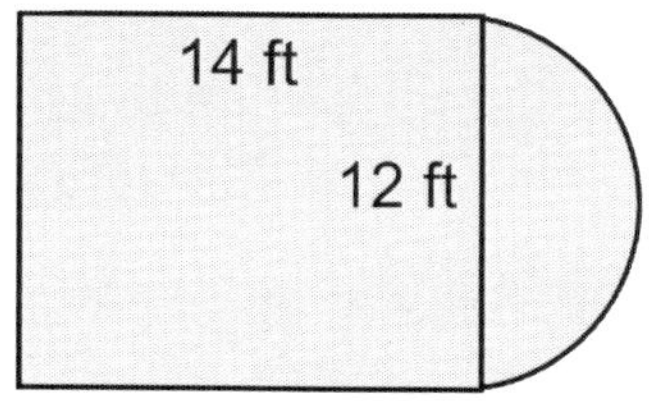

54) Jolly bought 5 bags of almond flour each weighing two tenth kg. She re packed into three bags to share them with her sisters. Find the weight of each re packed bag of flour

55) Write an equation and then find the value of x in the below

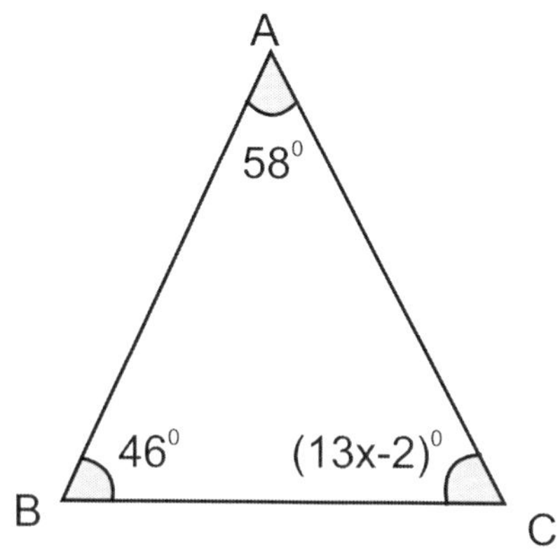

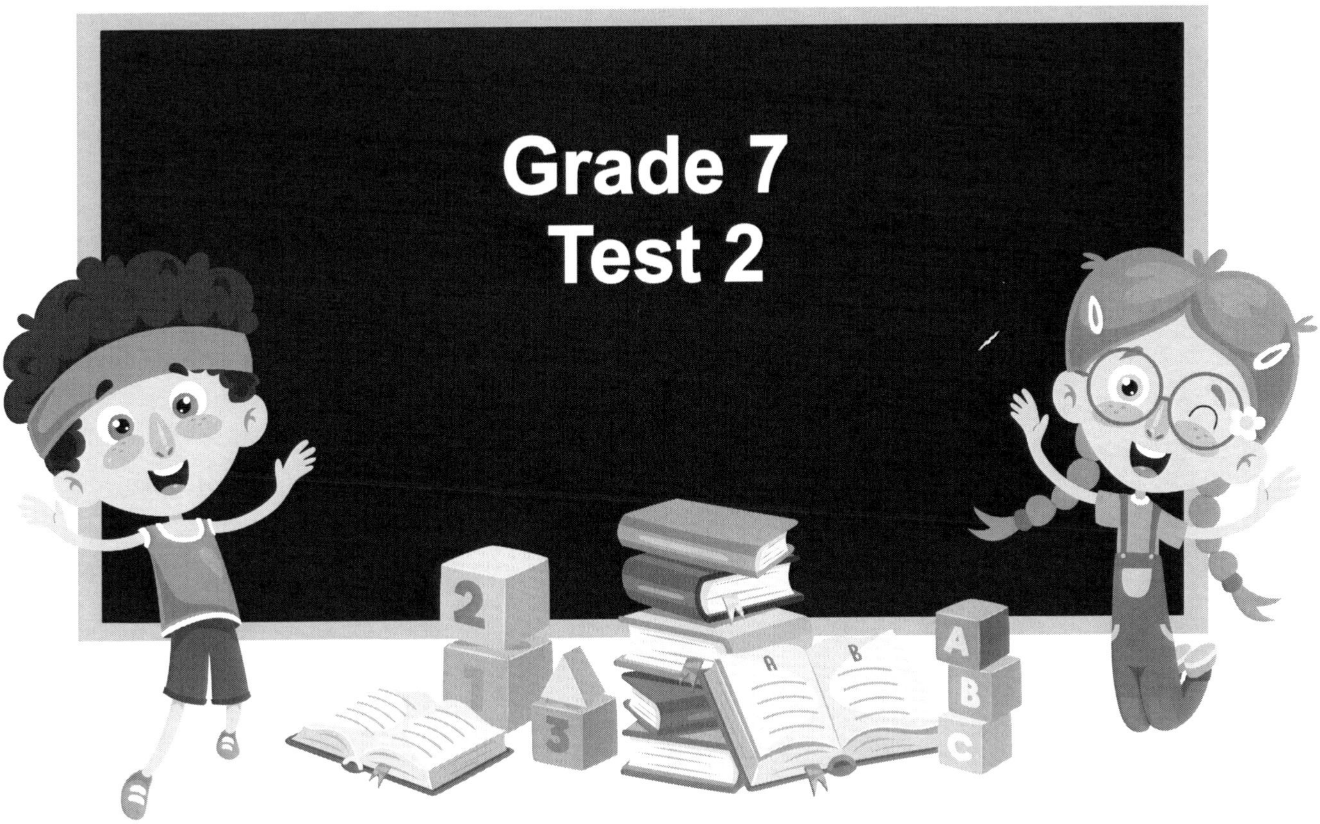
Grade 7
Test 2

1) Simplify the below

(15 - (-5)) ÷ (6 - 4)

(A) 10 (B) 6

(C) 0 (D) 13

2) Express the below number in scientific notation

74600

(A) 74.6×10^5 (B) 74.6×10^{-5}

(C) 7.46×10^5 (D) 7.46×10^4

3) Maria reduced the size of a photo to a width of 6 in. What is the new height if it was originally 28 in tall and 42 in wide ?

(A) 42 in (B) 4 in

(C) 1 in (D) 196 in

4) Simplify

$18 - (10 - (-9)^2)$

(A) 78 (B) 96

(C) 89 (D) 94

5) Find the volume of the cylinder with a radius of 6 m and a height of 4m.

(A) 388 m^3 (B) 384.5 m^3

(C) 334.5 m^3 (D) 452.4 m^3

6) Find the area of the enclosure.

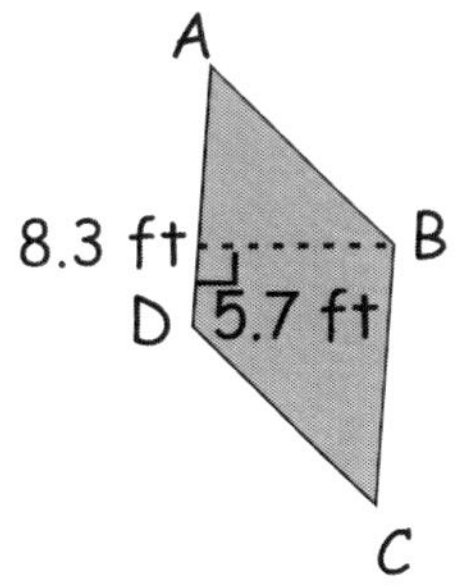

(A) 52.71 ft^2 (B) 23.7 ft^2

(C) 47.31 ft^2 (D) 94.62 ft^2

7) Find the total surface area of the given three dimensional shape.

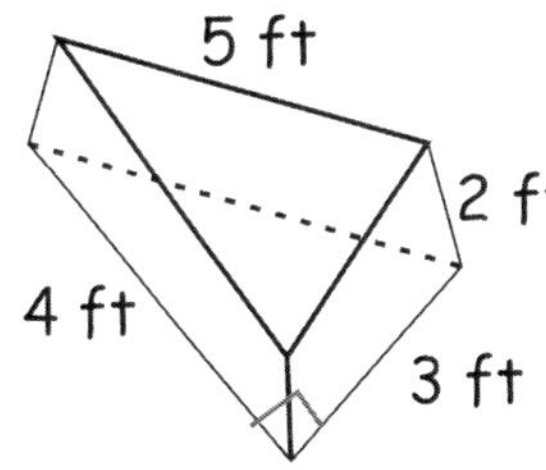

(A) 33.7 ft^2 (B) 27.6 ft^2

(C) 30..6 ft^2 (D) 36 ft^2

8) A class has 20 boys and 15 girls. If one representative from each sex has to be chosen, in how many ways this can be done ?

(A) 400 (B) 300

(C) 425 (D) 350

9) Find the median for the given below data.
45 , 57 , 52 , 52 , 53 , 42 , 49 , 53 , 51 , 43

(A) 51.5 (B) 50.5

(C) 52.5 (D) 45.5

10) Find the mean age from the following data.

Score	Frequency
31	1
42	1
44	2
45	1
48	1
49	3
50	1
51	2
52	4
53	3
54	3

(A) 50

(B) 48.66

(C) 47.36

(D) 49.18

11) Translate the verbal expression to an algebraic expression.
Half of n is less than or equal to 35.

(A) $2 - n \le 35$ (B) $n^2 \le 35$

(C) $\frac{n}{2} \le 35$ (D) $n - 2 \le 35$

12) Which of the following is the correct statement for the given expression ?

$8^x > 47$

(A) 8 decreased by x is greater than 47

(B) 8 to the x is greater than 47

(C) x times 8 is greater than 47

(D) 8 less than x is greater than 47

13) A cake recipe needs 3 cups of milk. Susan accidentally added 8 cups of milk.
How many more cups did she put in ?

(A) 2 (B) 1

(C) 4 (D) 5

14) Noah and his best friend got a cash prize. They split the money evenly, each getting $23.76. How much money was the cash prize ?

(A) $47.52 (B) $48.17

(C) $11.88 (D) $51.80

15) Write an equation showing the relation between x & y.

x	y
1	3
2	6
3	9
6	18

(A) $y = x + 2$

(B) $y = 2x$

(C) $y = 3x$

(D) $y = x + 3$

16) The table below shows goals made by Ben in his soccer tournament.
8 , 9 , 7 , 3 , 8

The teacher missed to add a student score. If the median and mode of the data is same. What is the missing score ?

(A) 8 (B) 5

(C) 10 (D) 9

17) A writing desk is priced at $249.50 and the discount offered on it is 55%, calculate the selling price.

(A) $112.27 (B) $137.23

(C) $112.28 (D) $386.73

18) Lucy is drawing a picture with a height of 2 in. The original picture had width of 2 in and a length of 4 in. What is the length of Lucy's drawing ?

(A) 2 in (B) 8 in

(C) 4 in (D) 3 in

19) The number 1.56×10^{-2} is equivalent to

(A) 156 (B) 0.0156

(C) 0.156 (D) 0.00156

20) Parallelogram ABCD and LMNO are congruent. Then what is the ratio of length $\overline{GH}$ to length $\overline{CD}$?

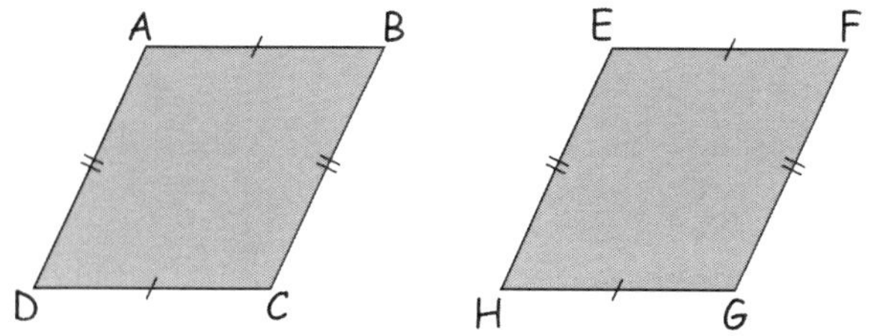

(A) 1 : 1 (B) 2 : 1

(C) 2 : 3 (D) 1 : 4

21) Find the value of p from the below triangles.

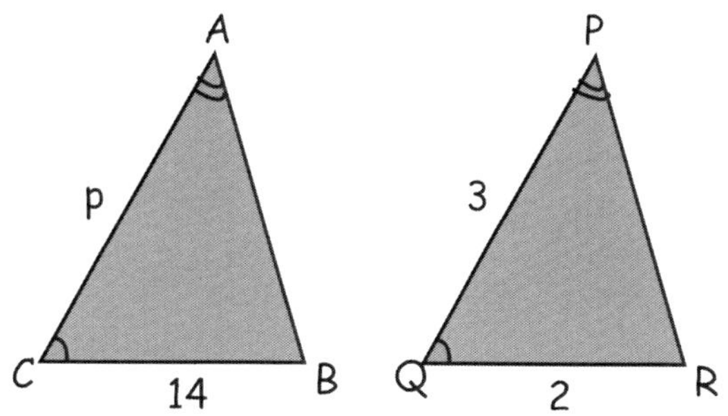

(A) $\frac{p}{14} = \frac{3}{2}$ (B) $\frac{p}{14} = \frac{5}{3}$

(C) $\frac{14}{p} = \frac{3}{2}$ (D) 14p = 6

22) Tracy takes $2500 debt every year for four years to pay his college fees. How much is Tracy's debt at the end of 4 years ? (Assuming no interest on the loan amount)

(A) 5000 (B) -10000

(C) -2500 (D) 10000

23) If you roll three normal, six-sided dice in a completely random manner, what is the probability that the three numbers that come up on the dice will all be identical ?

(A) $\frac{1}{36}$ (B) $\frac{1}{12}$

(C) $\frac{1}{18}$ (D) $\frac{1}{216}$

24) A local smoothie shop donates 5% of its sales of every Friday to a local charity. Based on the information given

(A) Total sales amount of last Friday was $37 and donated $750

(B) Total sales amount of last Friday was $100 and donated $95

(C) Total sales amount of last Friday was $750 and donated $37.50

(D) Total sales amount of last Friday was $250 and donated $125

A robot manufacturing company spends \$2880k every year as given in the pie chart below. Answer the questions 26 - 31.

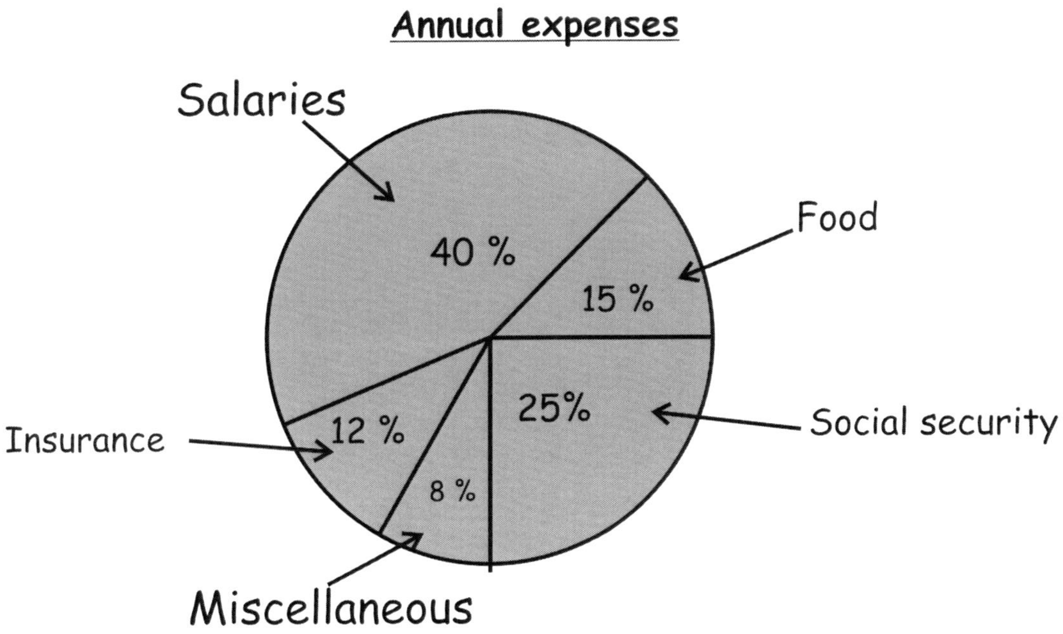

25) Find the amount was spent towards salaries ?

(A) \$1152k (B) \$1252k

(C) \$1100k (D) \$1052k

26) How much money is saved if the budget allocated to miscellaneous is not spent and food went 10% over the budget ?

(A) \$1972k (B) \$187.2k

(C) \$2736k (D) \$2076k

27) How much money was spent on food ?

(A) 432k (B) 335k

(C) 444k (D) 533k

28) How much money was spent on insurance ?

(A) 349k (B) 395.9k

(C) 312.6k (D) 345.6k

29) How much more money was spent on social security than insurance ?

(A) 377.38k (B) 384.49k

(C) 374.4k (D) 399.99k

30) Find the ratio between the amount spent on food and social security ?

(A) 2:5 (B) 5:3

(C) 3:5 (D) 2:3

31) The average test scores of grade 8 students are plotted as the box and whisker plot

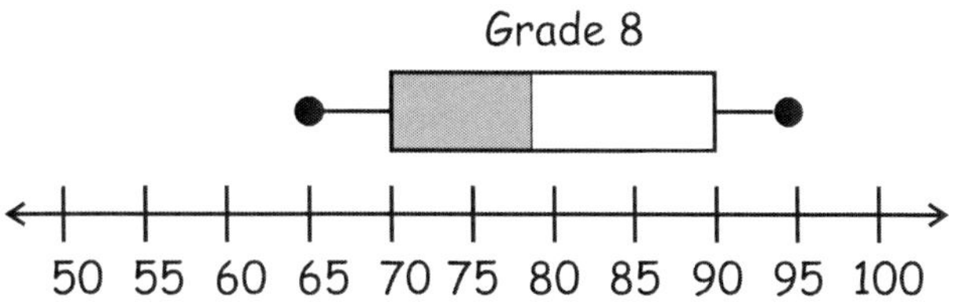

Find the range of the test scores based on the above data

(A) 20 (B) 45

(C) 30 (D) 35

32) Find the volume of the below figure

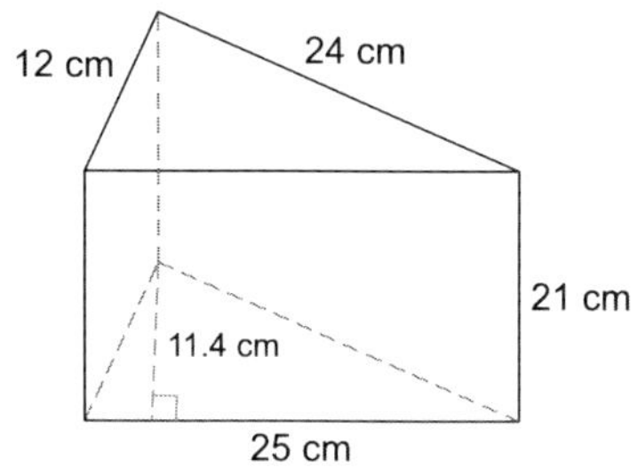

A) $2992.5\ cm^3$ B) $3351.6\ cm^3$

C) $3921.4\ cm^3$ D) $7842.8\ cm^3$

33) Solve the below equation

$$485 = -19 + 18r$$

A) $\{-36\}$ B) $\{28\}$

C) $\{-34\}$ D) $\{-13\}$

34) Simplify the below expression

$$8.8 + 9.6\ (k + 5.5)$$

A) $-9.09 + 10.6208k$

B) $61.6 + 9.6k$

C) $-9.09 + 4.7608k$

D) $0.61 + 4.7608k$

35) Simplify the below expression

$$\frac{9}{5}m - \frac{4}{5}\left(m + \frac{39}{7}\right)$$

A) $-\frac{52}{5}m - \frac{217}{15}$

B) $\frac{10}{9} - \frac{919}{180}m$

C) $\frac{31}{8}m - \frac{156}{35}$

D) $m - \frac{156}{35}$

36) Evaluate the below using the values given.

$$\frac{r}{6} - r(r + p) \text{ Given : } p = -4, \text{ and } r = 12$$

A) -107 B) -104

C) -94 D) -110

37) Solve the below equation

$$-5 = \frac{-20 + x}{2}$$

A) $\{10\}$ B) $\{-12\}$

C) $\{28\}$ D) $\{-21\}$

38) Solve the below inequality

$$-4 < \frac{n - 8}{3}$$

A) $n > -39$ B) $n < -4$

C) $n > -33$ D) $n > -4$

39) A square prism measuring 14 km along each edge of the base and 15 km tall. Find the surface area.

A) 1084.2 km^2 B) 1232 km^2

C) 2472 km^2 D) 1236 km^2

40) Simplify the below expression

$$-(-8 + 4n) - 13(2 + 6n)$$

A) $148 + 140n$ B) $27 - 143n$

C) $130 + 140n$ D) $-18 - 82n$

41) Find the value of x

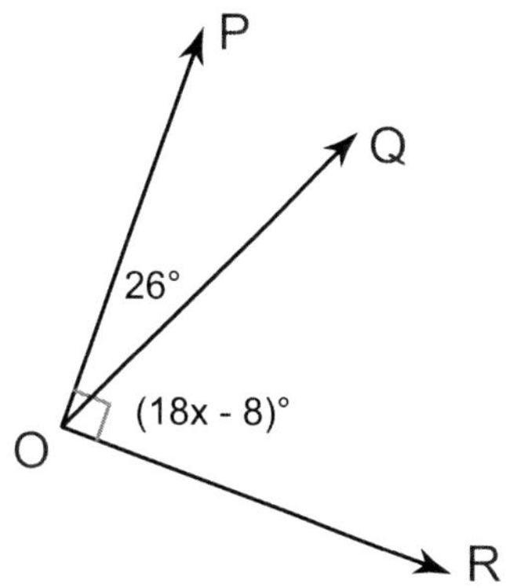

A) 14 B) 31

C) 4 D) 19

42) A rectangular prism measuring 13 in and 12 in along the base and 6 in tall. Find the volume

A) 4380.4 in^3 B) 936 in^3

C) 1872 in^3 D) 2190.2 in^3

43) Find the value of x

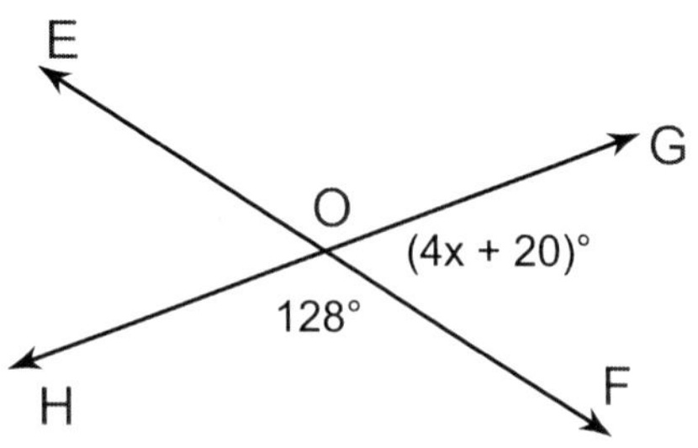

A) 8 B) 0

C) 2 D) -8

44) Evaluate the below using the values give

$\frac{z}{2} + y \times \frac{x}{4}$ Given : $x = -4$, $y = 20$, and $z = -10$

A) −10 B) −40

C) −13 D) −25

45) One lime costs \$0.33. How many limes can you buy for \$8.25?

46) Amy bought one seedless watermelon for \$1.89. How many seedless watermelons can Julio buy if he has \$18.90?

47) Find the distance between Yorkshire and Santa Cruz if they are 8 in apart on a map with a scale of 1 in : 20 mi.

48) The currency in the United Arab Emirates is the Dirham. The exchange rate is approximately $1 for every 3.7 Dirhams. At this rate, how many dollars would you get if you exchanged 17.8 Dirhams?

49) The currency in the United Arab Emirates is the Dirham. The exchange rate is approximately 3.7 Dirhams for every $1. At this rate, how many Dirhams would you get if you exchanged $3.10?

50) Which two measures are equal in the two data sets provided below

# of words in fiction book titles

3	3	2	3	4	4	2	5
3	3	1	2	2	2	2	

# of words in non-fiction book titles

6	2	6	1	6	5	2	3
2	2	2	2	5	2	5	4

(A) Median is same

(B) Mean and mode values are same

(C) Mean is same

(D) Mode is same

51) Which two measures are equal in the two data sets provided below

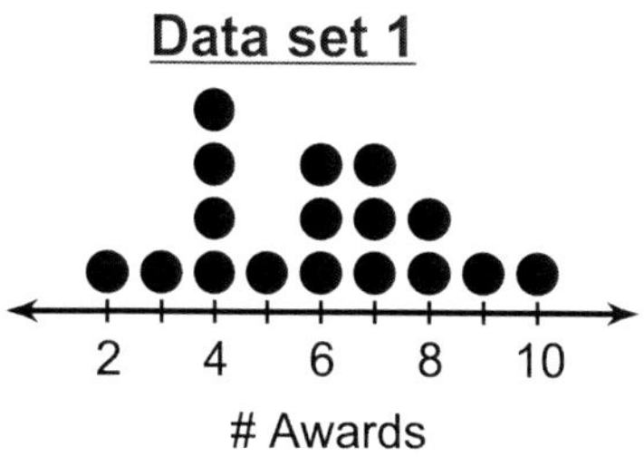

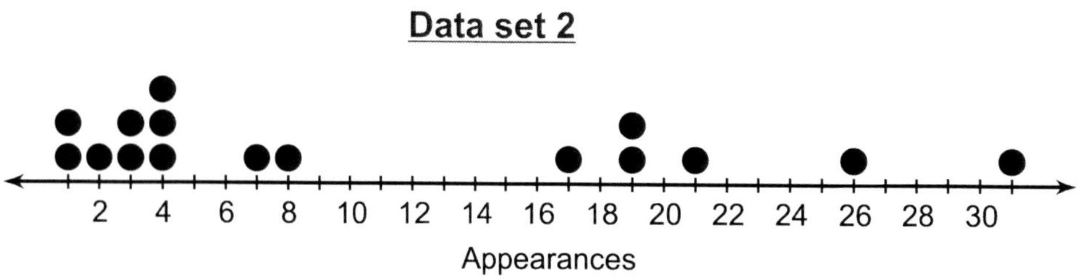

(A) Mean value is same in both data sets

(B) Median of set 1 is 0.5 more than set 2

(C) Median of set 1 is 0.5 less than set 2

(D) Median and mean are same

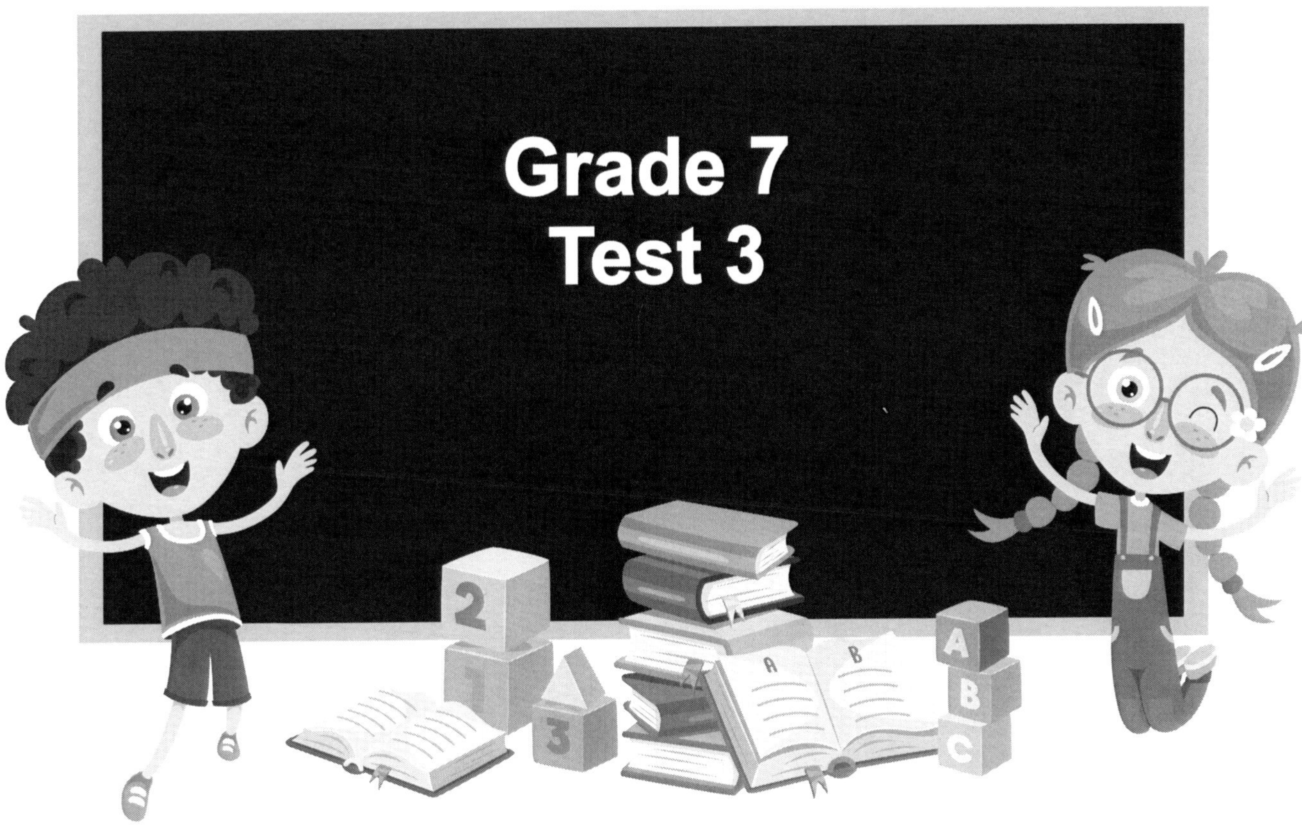
Grade 7
Test 3

1) Simplify the below

$$(5 - 11) \cdot 11 \div (-2)$$

(A) 78 (B) 92

(C) 93 (D) 83

2) Express the below number in scientific notation

0.0000085

(A) 0.85×10^{-6} (B) 85×10^{6}

(C) 8.5×10^{6} (D) 8.5×10^{-6}

3) If you can buy five seedless watermelons for \$9, then how many can you buy with \$18 ?

(A) 32 (B) 9

(C) 10 (D) 8

4) Simplify

$$15(17 - ((-21) \div (-3)))$$

(A) 150 (B) 148

(C) 162 (D) 156

5) Find the volume of the cylinder with a radius of 5 mi and a height of 4 mi.

(A) 70.7 mi^3 (B) 314.2 mi^3

(C) 78.6 mi^3 (D) 157.1 mi^3

6) Find the area of the enclosure.

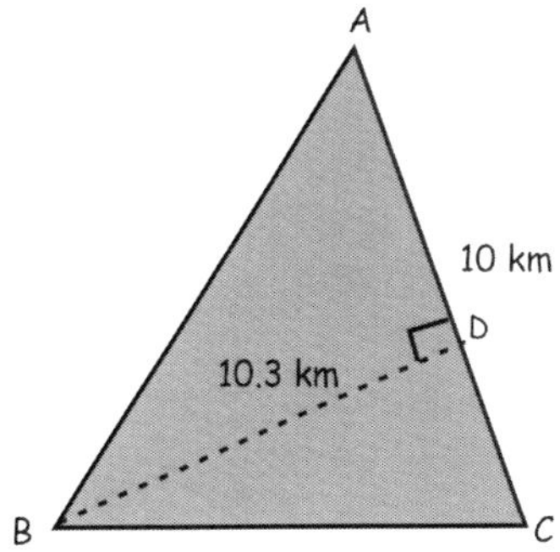

(A) 51.5 km^2 (B) 25.8 km^2

(C) 103 km^2 (D) 53.5 km^2

7) Find the total surface area of the given three dimensional shape.

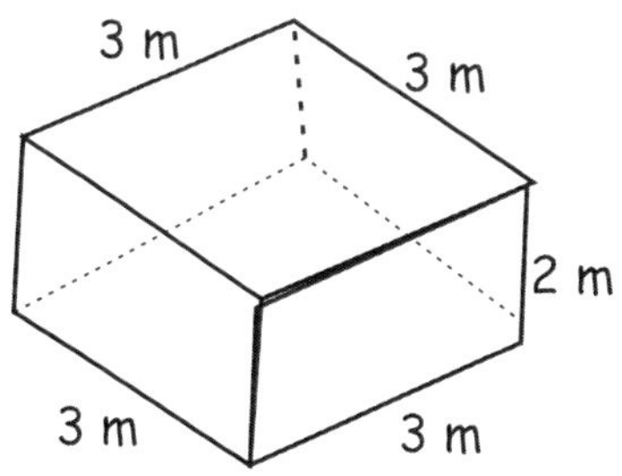

(A) 42 m^2 (B) 34 m^2

(C) 24 m^2 (D) 39 m^2

8) How many different outcomes arise from first tossing a coin and then rolling a die ?

(A) 12 (B) 10

(C) 8 (D) 14

9) Find the median for the given below data.
25.1 , 33 , 41.3 , 21.9 , 31.7 , 39 , 35.2 , 21.9 , 27 , 28.9 , 25.9

(A) 25.1 (B) 35.2

(C) 27 (D) 28.9

10) Find the mean of the following data.

Hours	Frequency
5.75	1
6.5	1
6.75	7
7	2
7.25	1
7.5	4
7.75	2
8	1
8.25	2
8	2

(A) 7.29

(B) 6.94

(C) 6.72

(D) 7.48

11) Translate the verbal expression to an algebraic expression.

The quotient of a number and 3 is equal to 15

(A) $\frac{3}{n}$ (B) n - 3 = 15

(C) $\frac{n}{3} = 15$ (D) $3^n = 15$

12) Charlie and seven of his friends went for dinner to a restaurant. They split evenly. Each person paid $10. What was the total bill ?

(A) $70 (B) $66

(C) $80 (D) $1.43

13) Last week Leo ran 8 miles less than Nathan. Leo ran 12 miles this week. How many miles did Nathan ran ?

(A) 18 (B) 20

(C) 4 (D) 28

14) Write an equation showing the relation between x & y.

x	y
6	30
8	28
10	16
16	20

(A) y = 6 + a

(B) y = 5a

(C) y = x + 30

(D) y = 36 - a

15) The table below shows number of brand A shirts sold across various stores.

259 , 234 , 252 , 266 , 267 , 269 , 259 , 237

If the median and mode of the data is not altered after adding the missing sales, what could be the missing sales value ?

(A) 268 (B) 235

(C) 266 (D) 259

16) David has a 5% discount coupon for any purchases at store A. All hand bags are priced at $99.99. What is the selling price of one bag ?

(A) $79.99 (B) $89.50

(C) $94.99 (D) $104.99

17) A box of cherries cost $2. How many boxes of cherries can Tom buy for $20 ?

(A) 10 (B) 40

(C) 11 (D) 9

18) The size of a certain type of molecule is 0.00009078 inch. If this number is expressed as 9.078×10^n, what is the value of n ?

(A) -5 (B) -8

(C) 5 (D) 8

19) Which of the below is greater than 325% ?

(A) $3\frac{29}{100}$ (B) $\frac{4}{13}$

(C) $3\frac{1}{4}$ (D) 325

20) Circle 'A' and Circle 'B' are congruent and their radii are congruent by a scale factor of 4. Then what is the ratio of their areas ?

(A) 1 : 4 (B) 1 : 16

(C) 2 : 3 (D) 1 : 2

21) Find the value of n from the below triangles.

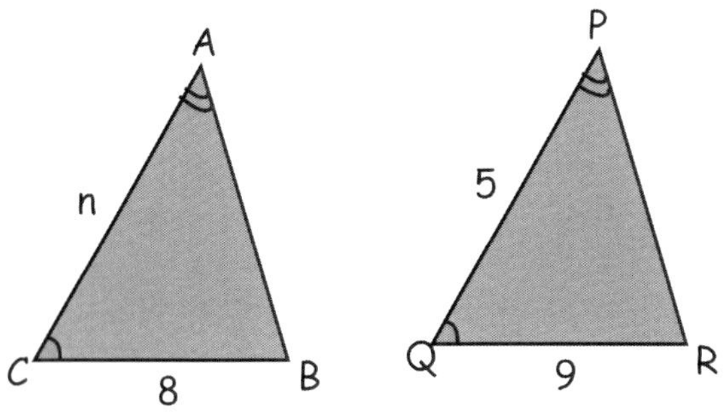

(A) $8n = 72$

(B) $\frac{n}{8} = \frac{5}{9}$

(C) $\frac{8}{n} = \frac{5}{9}$

(D) $\frac{n}{8} = \frac{9}{5}$

22) A submarine is 1050 meters below the sea level. Later it ascended 300 meters, But then descended another 275 meters and finally stopped at this location. Where was the submarine in relation to sea level when it stopped ?

(A) 1625

(B) -1625

(C) 1025

(D) -1025

23) Below equation is an example of

31 * (21 + 51) = 31 * 21 + 31 * 51

(A) Identity Property of Multiplication

(B) Associative Property of Addition

(C) Distributive Property

(D) Commutative Property of Multiplication

24) Two six sided dice are rolled. What is the probability of getting a score greater than 4 ?

(A) $\frac{32}{36}$

(B) $\frac{31}{36}$

(C) $\frac{1}{6}$

(D) $\frac{5}{6}$

25) A certain game spinner has eight equal-sized sections numbered 1, 2, 3, 2, 4, 3, 2 and 5. If you spin this spinner twice (randomly - no cheating!), what is the probability that you will get a two both times ?

(A) $\frac{3}{8}$

(B) $\frac{6}{8}$

(C) $\frac{9}{64}$

(D) $\frac{9}{16}$

26) A local bakery donates 10% of its sales of every Saturday to a local charity. Based on the information given

(A) Total sales amount of last Friday was $950 and donated $100

(B) Total sales amount of last Friday was $165 and donated $1650

(C) Total sales amount of last Friday was $770 and donated $70

(D) Total sales amount of last Friday was $1650 and donated $165

27) The cost of a chair is $249.50 and a 5% of tax is added to it. Calculate the selling price

(A) $237.55 (B) $274.25

(C) $261.98 (D) $12.48

The annual expenditure of an average house hold in the Washington DC is given in the below pie chart. Answer the questions 28 - 33

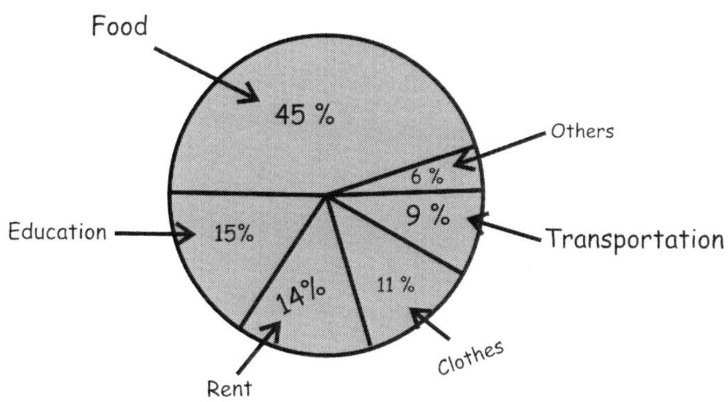

28) Find the ratio of expenses made on education and food ?

(A) 3:1 (B) 1:3

(C) 2:5 (D) 2:3

29) Find the ratio of expenses made on rent and others ?

(A) 7:3 (B) 3:7

(C) 5:7 (D) 7:2

30) Find the ratio of expenses made on clothes and transportation ?

(A) 1:11 (B) 6:11

(C) 11:9 (D) 9:11

31) Tony's annual income is $25,000. Find the amount spent on rent and food ?

(A) $17,250 (B) $16,750

(C) $11,250 (D) $14,750

32) Tony's annual income is $25,000. Find the amount spent on rent and clothes ?

(A) $6,250 (B) $6,575

(C) $6,650 (D) $7,625

33) Tony's annual income is $25,000. Find the amount spent on education ?

(A) $3,350 (B) $3,880

(C) $3,745 (D) $3,750

34) Simplify the below expression

$$2\left(b+\frac{39}{7}\right)+\frac{7}{5}$$

A) $2b+\frac{439}{35}$

B) $\frac{29}{6}b+\frac{1931}{140}$

C) $-\frac{8}{9}-\frac{203}{90}b$

D) $2b+\frac{1931}{140}$

35) Simplify the below expression

$$5(11+9n)-17(-17n-10)$$

A) $225+334n$ B) 81

C) 67 D) 63

36) Simplify the below expression

$$-13(b+3)+18(4b+5)$$

A) $79b+45$ B) $59b+45$

C) $28b+144$ D) $59b+51$

37) Find the volume of the below figure

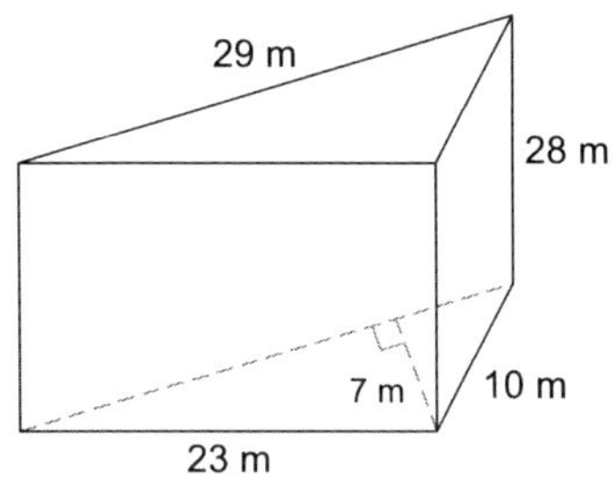

A) 6252.4 m³ B) 3126.2 m³

C) 12504.8 m³ D) 2842 m³

38) Solve the below equation

$$-21 = \frac{x}{2} - 10$$

A) −20 B) 16

C) −22 D) −27

39) Solve the below equation

$$6 - 5k = 71$$

A) −20 B) 40

C) 28 D) −13

40) Evaluate the below using the values given.

$$m - p + \frac{m+q}{4}$$

Given : $m = 9$, $p = -16$, and $q = 19$

A) 28 B) 50 C) 52 D) 32

41) Evaluate the below using the values given.

$$x + 2\left(yx + z\right)$$

Given : $x = 15$, $y = -4$, and $z = -19$

A) −125 B) −143

C) −146 D) −161

42) Find the value of x.

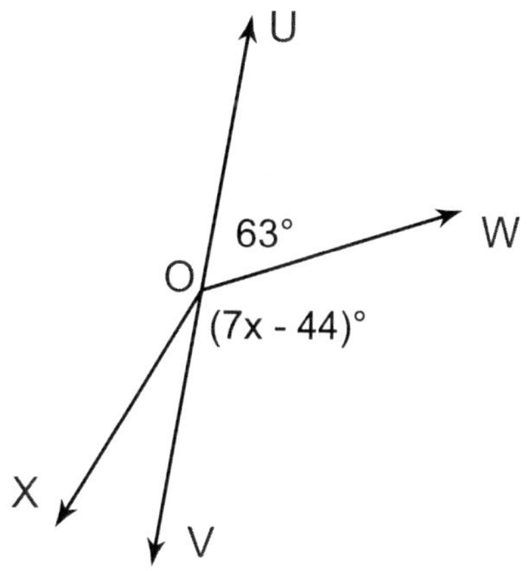

A) 39 B) 27

C) 23 D) 22

43) Find the value of x.

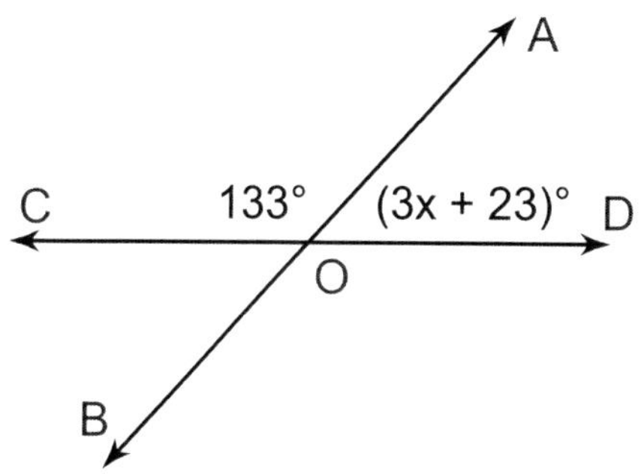

A) 30 B) 10

C) 8 D) 24

44) Solve the below inequality

$12 - 3r \geq 81$

A) $r \geq 5$ B) $r \geq -66$

C) $r \geq -23$ D) $r \leq -23$

45) A square prism measuring 3 in along each edge of the base and 7 in tall. Find the surface area.

A) 102 in² B) 367.2 in²

C) 408 in² D) 204 in²

46) A rectangular prism measuring 2 m and 9 m along the base and 5 m tall. Find the volume

A) 52.2 m³ B) 45 m³

C) 57.9 m³ D) 90 m³

47) Find the value of x.

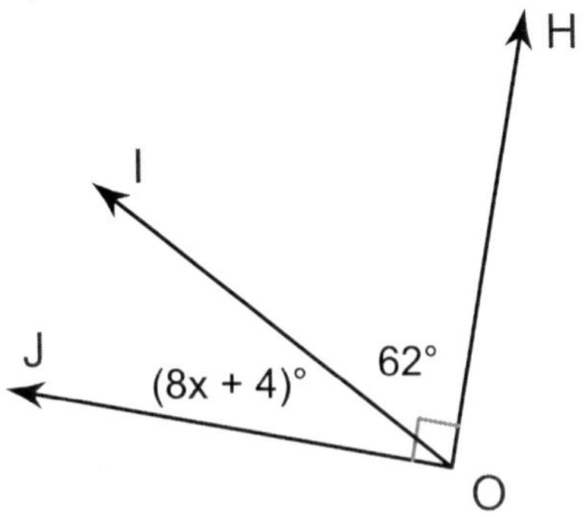

A) 3 B) 23

C) 24 D) 7

48) Find the value of x.

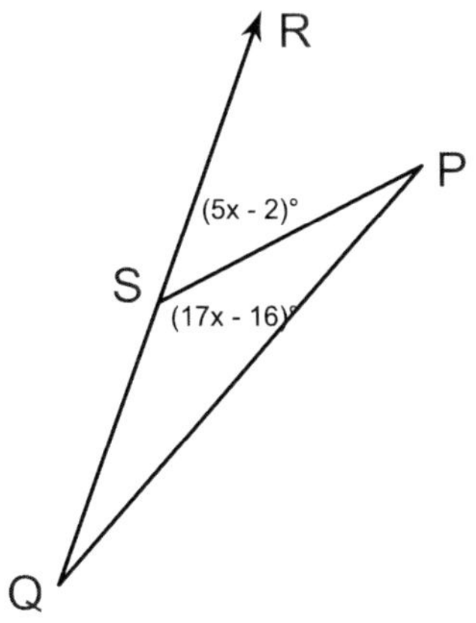

A) -29 B) 9

C) -11 D) -25

49) One honey tangerine costs $0.70. How many tangerines can you buy for $19.60?

50) Find the distance between Madison and Yorkshire if they are 7 in apart on a map with a scale of 1 in : 20 mi.

51) Find the mode and median for the below data set

32	52	47	43	52	55	36
57	50	51	47	50	51	51
50						

52) Find the mean and median for the below data set

1	8	6	12	5	13	15
4	19	18	6	3	8	12
6	10					

53) In a school president pole survey 3 out of 5 voters are supporting Sam. There are 325 students participated in voting. How many people have voted for Sam?

54) Write an equation and then find the value of x in the below

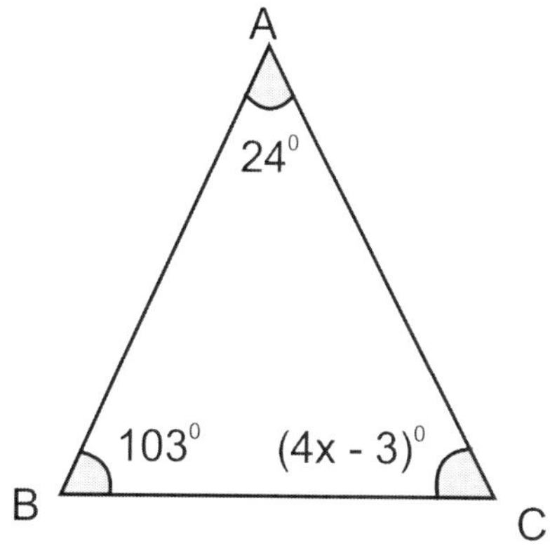

55) Find the mode, median, and mean
for the below data set.

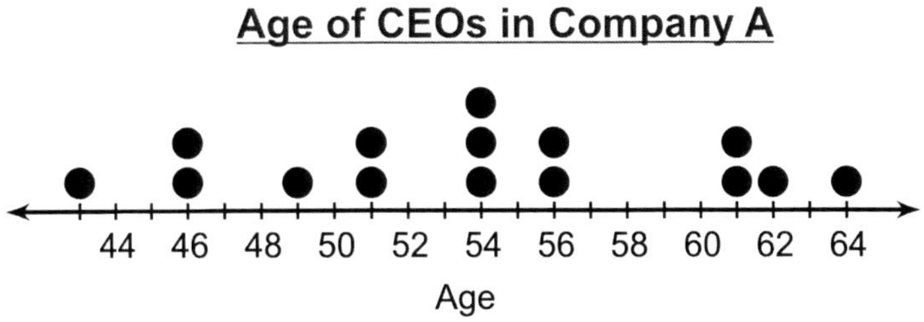

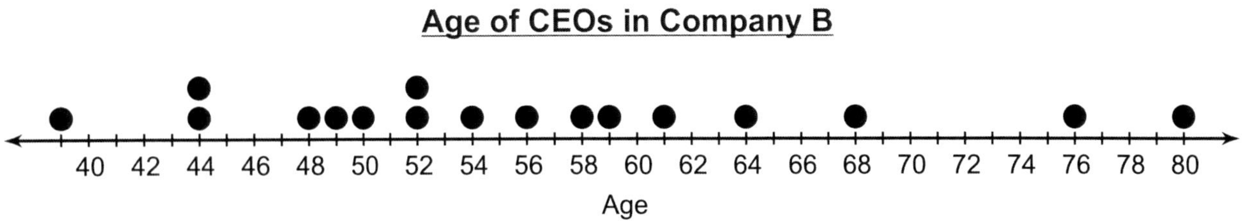

(A) Mean is same

(B) Mode is same

(C) Median and mean are same

(D) Median is same

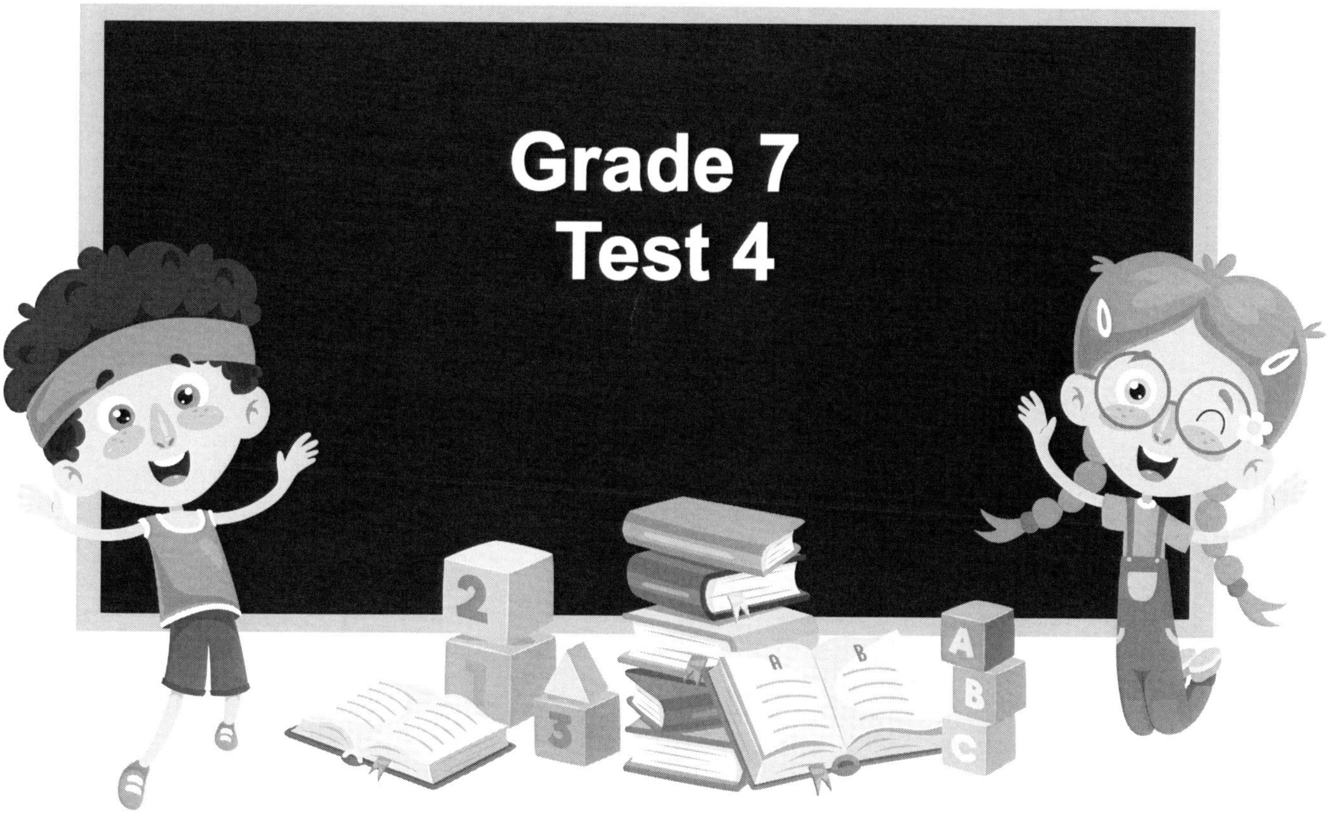
Grade 7
Test 4

1) Simplify the below expression

$$-\frac{13}{8}+\frac{5}{6}\left(\frac{1}{4}r+1\right)$$

A) $-\frac{32}{9}+\frac{23}{3}r$ B) $-\frac{19}{24}+\frac{5}{24}r$

C) $\frac{131}{36}r+\frac{3}{2}$ D) $\frac{50}{9}r-\frac{77}{54}$

2) Simplify the below expression

$$\frac{5}{6}\left(-\frac{1}{2}n+1\right)+1$$

A) $\frac{47}{70}n-\frac{31}{7}$ B) $\frac{5}{8}n-\frac{829}{280}$

C) $\frac{47}{70}n-\frac{219}{70}$ D) $\frac{11}{6}-\frac{5}{12}n$

3) Simplify the below expression

$$-3.1(1-7.63x)-9.9$$

A) $-13+23.653x$

B) $-15.05x-50.14$

C) $-15.05x-46.44$

D) $-15.15x-46.44$

4) Simplify the below expression

$$18(x+3)-(8x-16)$$

A) $10x+57$ B) $10x+76$

C) $156x-40$ D) $10x+70$

5) Simplify the below expression

$$-17(1+7n)-6(n-1)$$

A) $-164-40n$ B) $-11-140n$

C) $-11-125n$ D) $-164-24n$

6) Simplify the below expression

$$-5(x-20)+18(-10-10x)$$

A) $-189x-80$ B) $-206x-80$

C) $-185x-80$ D) $-206x-67$

7) Simplify the below expression

$$8(12 - x) + 15(15x + 12)$$

A) $-152x - 1$ B) $-152x + 8$

C) $276 + 217x$ D) $282 + 217x$

8) A rectangular prism measuring 13 km and 19 km along the base and 10 km tall.

A) 941.2 km^2 B) 1134 km^2

C) 550.6 km^2 D) 470.6 km^2

9) Evaluate the below using the values given.

$$\frac{z - z}{6} + x + z \quad \text{Given : } x = -9, \text{and} z = 5$$

A) −4 B) 6

C) −13 D) 16

10) Evaluate the below using the values given

$$r^2q - -\frac{3}{3} \quad \text{Given : } q = 8, \text{ and } r = -4$$

A) 124 B) 109

C) 119 D) 129

11) Solve the below equation

$$-23 = \frac{n - 6}{2}$$

A) −40 B) −37

C) 35 D) −33

12) Solve the below equation

$$2 \geq -2 + \frac{x}{6}$$

A) $x \leq -35$ B) $x \geq -55$

C) $x \leq -55$ D) $x \leq 24$

13) Solve the below equation

$$-10 = \frac{n}{5} - 15$$

A) −6 B) 25

C) 35 D) 38

14) Solve the below equation

$$\frac{p - 3}{26} \geq -1$$

A) $p \geq -23$ B) $p \leq -23$

C) $p \leq -55$ D) $p \leq 11$

15) Simplify the below expression

$\frac{p}{4} + q - 14p$ Given : $p = 4$, and $q = 18$

A) −42 B) −43

C) −41 D) −37

16) Find the value of x.

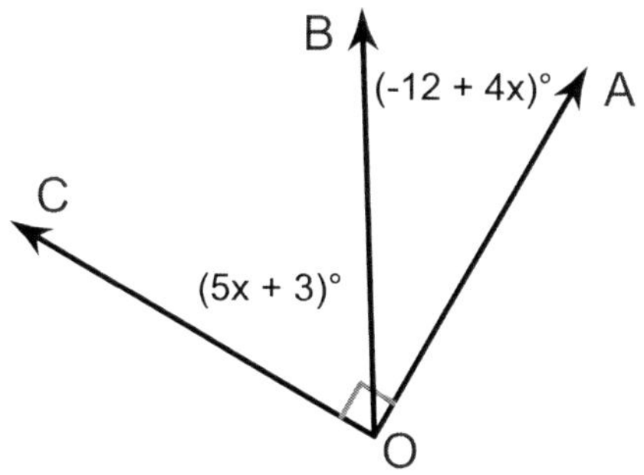

A) 31 B) 3

C) 11 D) 14

17) Find the value of x.

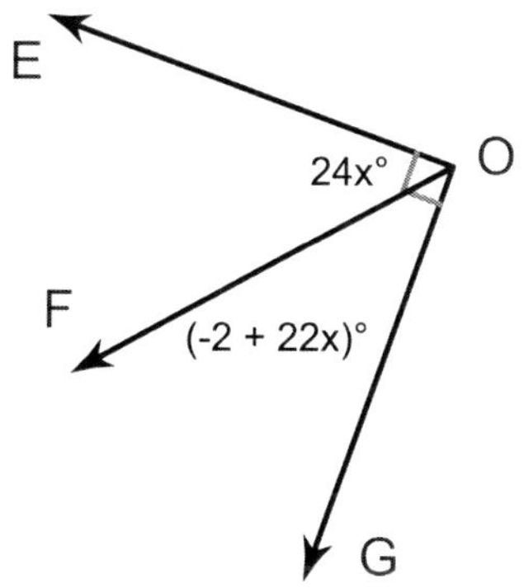

A) 15 B) 23

C) 2 D) 6

18) Find the value of x.

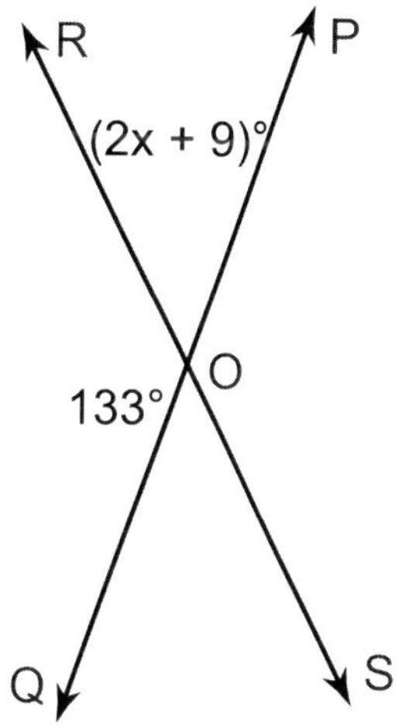

A) 19 B) 6

C) -1 D) -2

19) Find the value of x.

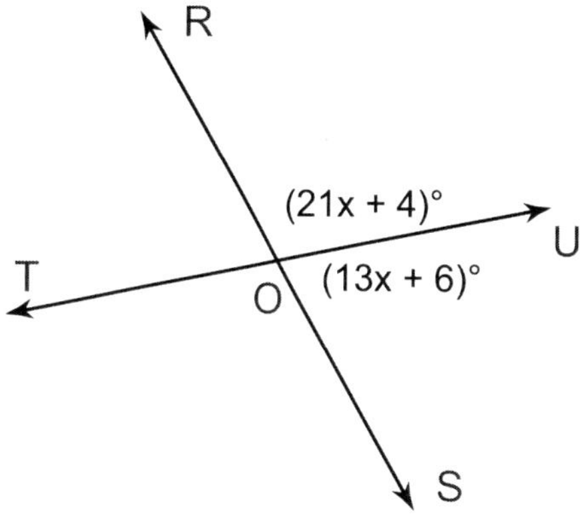

A) 5 B) 22

C) 32 D) 31

20) Find the value of x.

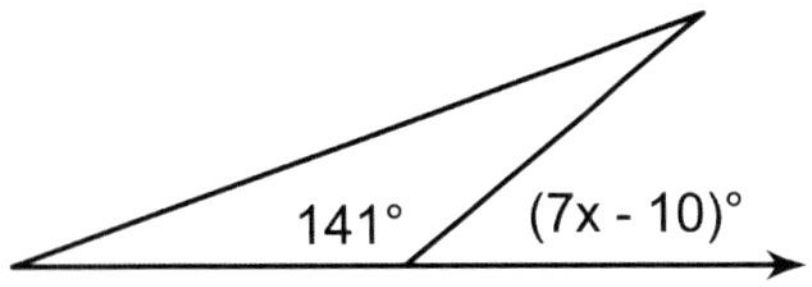

A) 5 B) 9

C) -13 D) 7

21) Find the value of x.

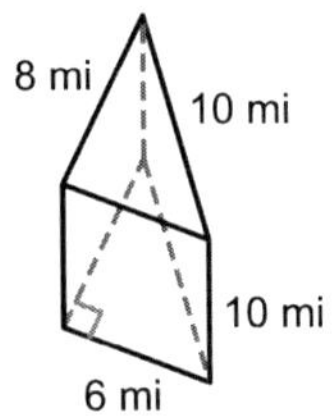

A) 192 mi^3 B) 145.3 mi^3

C) 240 mi^3 D) 169 mi^3

22) Find the surface area of the below figure.

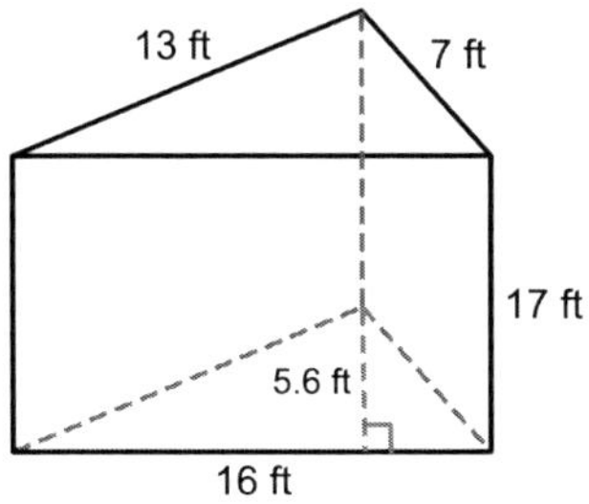

A) 701.6 ft^2 B) 1248.8 ft^2

C) 1411.1 ft^2 D) 1403.2 ft^2

23) A rectangular prism measuring 3 mi and 4 mi along the base and 5 mi tall.

A) 49.2 mi^3 B) 66.2 mi^3

C) 60 mi^3 D) 56.6 mi^3

24) A square prism measuring 9 km along each edge of the base and 14 km tall.

A) 963.9 km^3 B) 1134 km^3

C) 1638.6 km^3 D) 1927.8 km^3

25) If you can buy one bunch of cilantro for $1.60, then how many can you buy with $6.40?

26) One bunch of seedlees green grapes costs $2.50. How many bunches of seedless green grapes can you buy for $22.50?

27) Sam purchased 8 mangoes for $23.94 Find the unit price of the mango.

28) Zara purchased 3 pencils for $2.07 Find the unit price of the pencils.

29) Will took a trip to Tonga. Upon leaving he decided to convert all of his Pa'anga back into dollars. How many dollars did he receive if he exchanged 14.9 Pa'anga at a rate of 2.1 Pa'anga for $1?

30) Find the distance between Aldie and Potomac mills if they are 4 in apart on a map with a scale of 1 in : 5 mi.

31) Lola took a trip to Peru. Upon leaving she decided to convert all of her Soles back into dollars. How many dollars did she receive if she exchanged 11.8 Soles at a rate of $1 = 3.2 Soles?

32) Dan was planning a trip to K islands. The exchange rate is 3.2 kross for every $1. How many kross would he get if he exchanged $4.60?

33) A map has a scale of 1 cm : 6 km. If Baltimore and Greenwood are 24 km apart, then they are how far apart on the map?

34) Find the distance between Ashburn and Resturn on a map with a scale of 1 : 7 mi if they are actually 70 mi apart.

35) Compare the data measures of the below data sets

study hours

7.5	7.25	7	6.75	7	6.5
6.5	7.75	8	4.75	6	6.75
7.5	7	7.5	7		

study hours

4	5	4	6	7	7	7	7
4	6	7	5	7	6	6	

(A) Median is same

(B) Mean and mode values are same

(C) Mode is same

(D) Median and mean are same

36) Compare the data measures of the below data sets

Hits in a Round of Hacky Sack

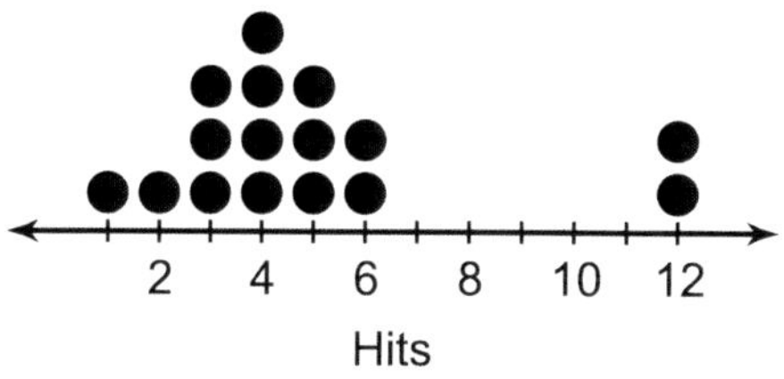

(A) Mean and median are same

(B) Median is greater than mean

(C) Mode is greater than median

(D) Median and mode are same

37) Area of square ABCD is 64 ft. If the side is increased by 25% what is the new area of square ABCD ?

38) Ian solves 8 out of 9 problems correctly. If he solves 189 problems this week find the probability of incorrect problems

39) Jack finds 6 out of 7 boxes are good in todays shipment that was delivered. The total number orders delivered are 1414. Find the probability of spoiled mango boxes.

40) Which equation fits the below data?

x	y
20	13
13	6
5	-2
6	-1

(A) x = y - 7

(B) x - y = 7

(C) x - y = -7

(D) x = y + 6

41) Which equation fits the below data?

x	y
5	25
7	49
9	81
13	169

(A) $y = x^2$

(B) y = x + 20

(C) y = 5x

(D) y = 13x

42) Find the area of the below figure.

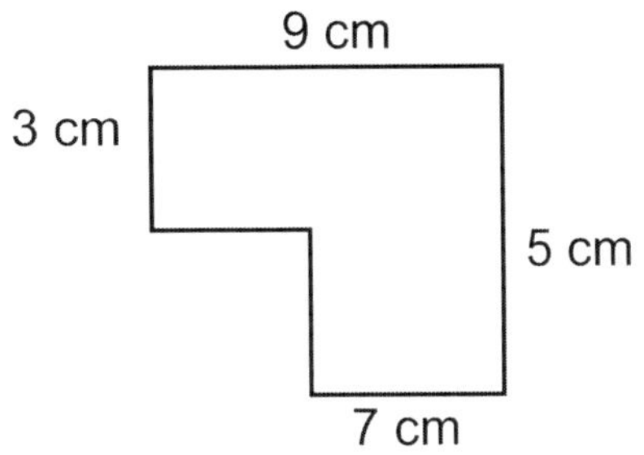

43) Find the average of the below data

38 , 29 , 34 , 35 , 24

44) Zacky Zen lab has new cells for drug testing. If each cell is 0.00000079 inches in diameter, what is 0.00000079 written in scientific notation?

(A) 7.9×10^{-6} (B) 0.79×10^{-9}

(C) 7.9×10^{-8} (D) 7.9×10^{-7}

45) Paul, the show polisher, polishes one pair of shoes in 2 min. At this rate how many shoe pairs can he polish in one-fourth of an hour completely?

46) Rita has 4 pants,3 shirts and 2 pairs of shoes. How many different outfits can she make choosing one from each

(A) 20 (B) 24

(C) 9 (D) 16

47) ABC painting company charges \$10 for every sq.ft of painting. Oliver wants to paint 2 rooms in his house. Area of each room is 800 sq.ft. How much does it cost him to paint?

(A) \$800 (B) \$8000

(C) \$200 (D) \$1600

48) Zacky lab is conducting a drug test. Thelab technicians observe that bacteria count is reduced to half every 44 minutes. At 12 PM January 4th 2024 the bacteria count was 800,000. How many bacteria cells are remaining at 7:24 PM on January 4th 2024?

49) Gia sells 5 scarfs at \$10 at a local fair. At this rate, how much does she make by selling 800 scarfs?

(A) \$500 (B) \$4000

(C) \$1600 (D) \$8000

50) Madam M branded bags are on sale. The store is offering 30% discount on original price of \$160 each pack. Find the discount amount offered.

(A) \$48 (B) \$82

(C) \$112 (D) \$102

51) Evaluate the below

$(5 + 3)^2 + (9 \div 3) - (9^2 + 3^2)$

52) Evaluate the below

$(44 \div 11)^2 + 7 \times 8 - 8$

53) Given a = 5, b = 1

Simplify 5 + a x 7 - b x 5

54) Which of the below sets has the lowest average value?

(A) {2,5,5,2,4} (B) {5,5,5,5,6}

(C) {9,8,7,4,10} (D) {1,1,3,4,5}

55) Write the equation and find the value of x

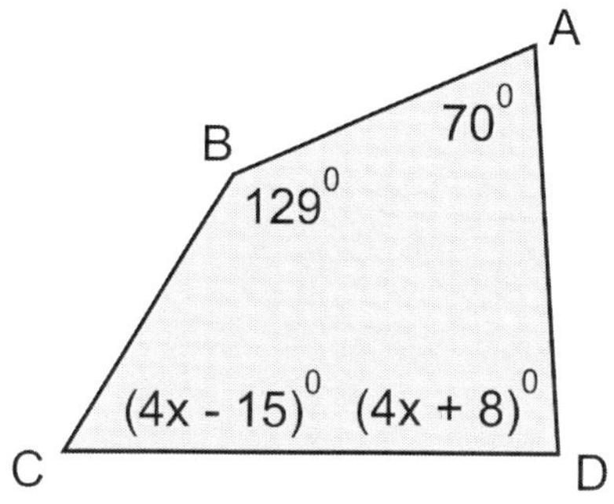

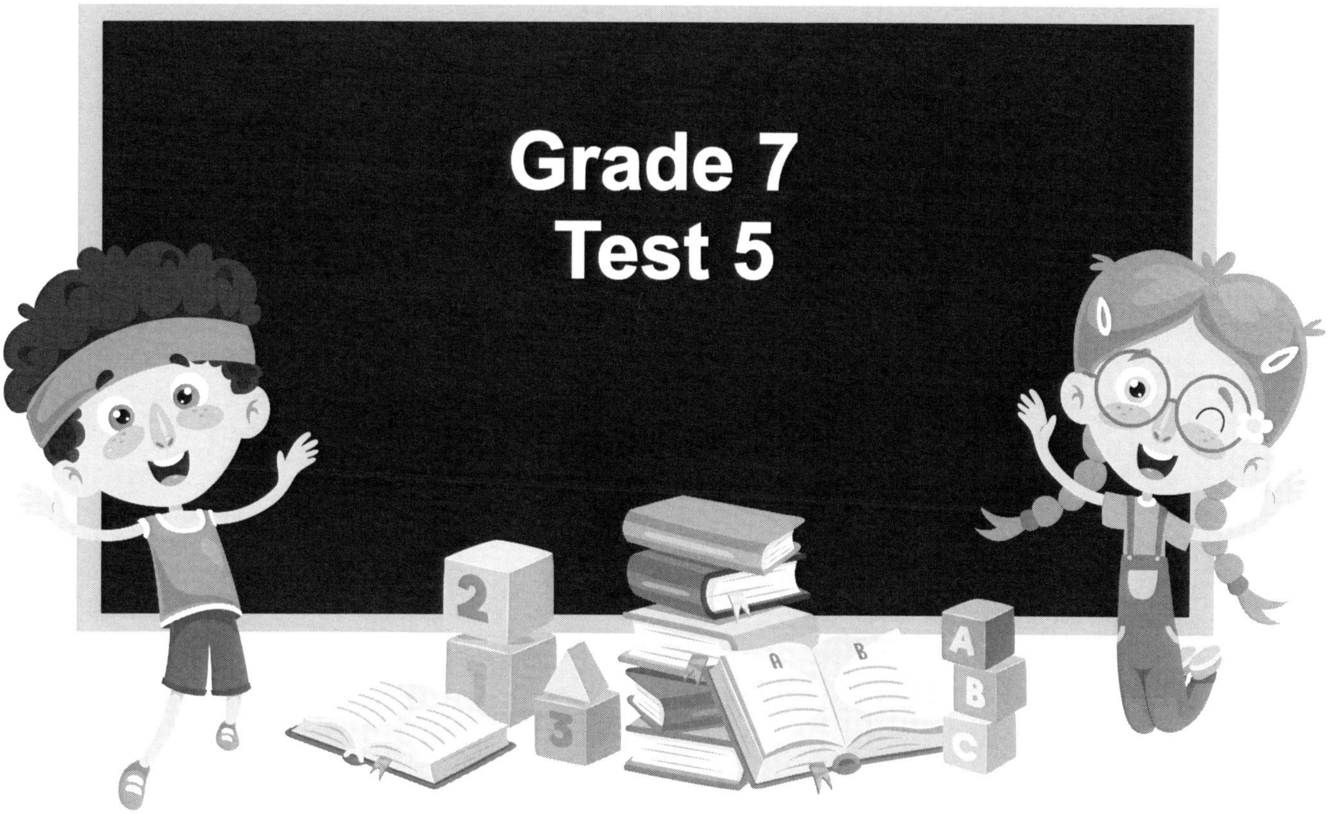
Grade 7
Test 5

1) Simplify the below expression

$6(15m-16)-6(m+14)$

A) $12-111m$ B) $21-111m$

C) $84m-180$ D) $345m-158$

2) Simplify the below expression

$-6(1-20b)+9(1+18b)$

A) $3+282b$

B) $-256+160b$

C) $-189b+301$

D) $-256+176b$

3) Simplify the below expression

$6.7-4.3(-7.03n+4.8)$

A) $-6.7+30.229n$

B) $-14.4+30.229n$

C) $-14.5+30.229n$

D) $-13.94+30.229n$

1) Simplify the below expression

$-10(-17-x)-4(6+3x)$

A) $20+46x$ B) $18+46x$

C) $146-2x$ D) $-98x+150$

4) Simplify the below expression

$\frac{37}{10}k-\frac{2}{3}\left(k+\frac{52}{5}\right)$

A) $\frac{379}{120}k-\frac{139}{15}$

B) $\frac{91}{30}k-\frac{104}{15}$

C) $\frac{341}{30}k+9$

D) $\frac{379}{120}k-\frac{104}{15}$

5) Simplify the below expression

$-\frac{33}{10}\left(\frac{3}{8}n+\frac{5}{2}\right)-2$

A) $-\frac{41}{4}-\frac{99}{80}n$

B) $\frac{907}{80}n-\frac{675}{56}$

C) $\frac{59}{6}-\frac{77}{8}n$

D) $-\frac{731}{56}+\frac{907}{80}n$

6) Simplify the below expression

$5(-n-2)+2(7n+17)$

A) $9n+24$ B) $-16+371n$

C) $-16+386n$ D) $9n+8$

7) Find the value of x.

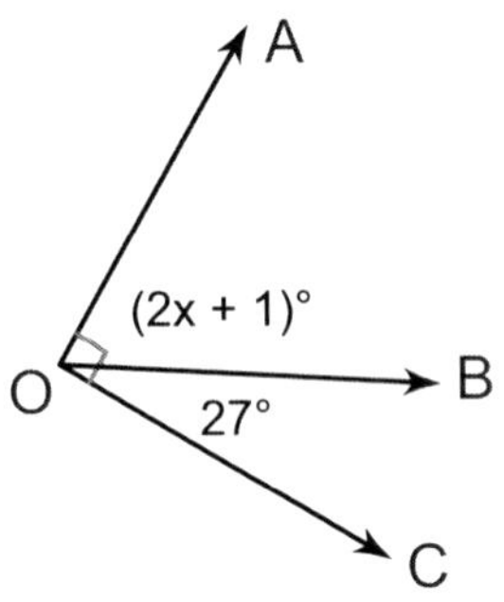

A) 49 B) 35

C) 31 D) 53

8) Find the value of x.

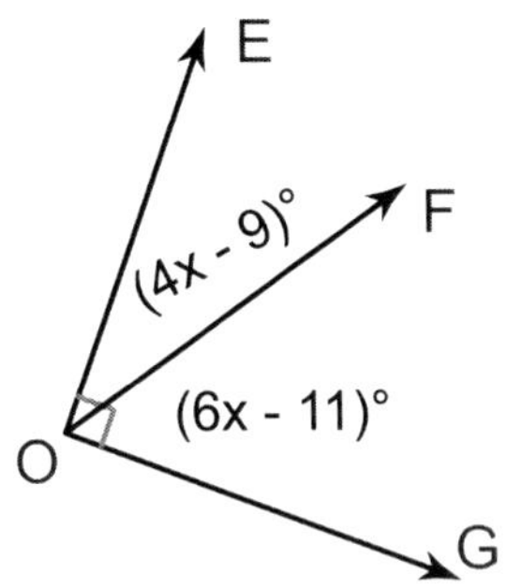

A) 11 B) 20

C) 21 D) 10

9) Solve the below equation.

$\frac{m-13}{2}=-5$

A) -35 B) 3

C) 18 D) 8

10) Solve the below inequality.

$-8(x+7)<-256$

A) $x>25$ B) $x<-16$

C) $x>-16$ D) $x<-43$

11) Solve the below inequality.

$6\le 5+\frac{v}{9}$

A) $v\ge 9$ B) $v\le -22$

C) $v\le 9$ D) $v\le -37$

12) Solve the below inequality.

$\frac{p-3}{2}=17$

A) 2 B) -19

C) 37 D) 15

13) Evaluate the below using the values given

$$mn \times \frac{p+10}{6}$$

Given : $m=-19$, $n=-5$, and $p=-16$

A) −105 B) −81

C) −98 D) −95

14) Evaluate the below using the values given

$$-7\left(z \times \frac{y}{6}+3\right)$$ Given : $y=12$, and $z=-4$

A) 20 B) 35

C) 39 D) 49

15) Evaluate the below using the values given

$$x\left(18+\frac{y}{4}\right)+x$$ Given : $x=4$, and $y=20$

A) 115 B) 100

C) 94 D) 96

16) Find the surface area of the below figure

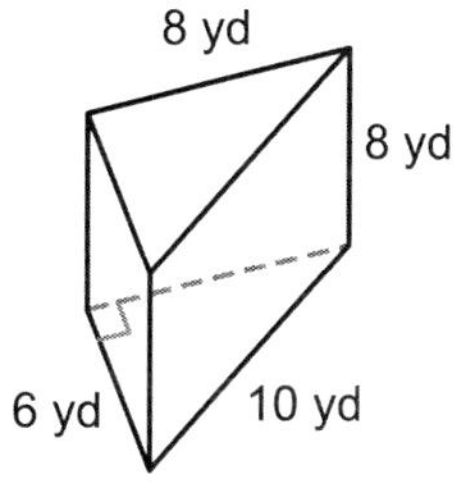

A) 120 yd² B) 240 yd²

C) 328.5 yd² D) 280.8 yd²

17) Find the volume of the below figure

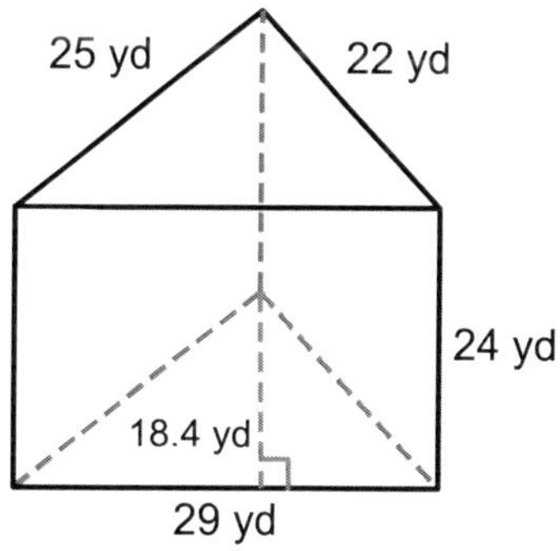

A) 5506.8 yd³ B) 2230.3 yd³

C) 4460.5 yd³ D) 6403.2 yd³

18) Find the value of x.

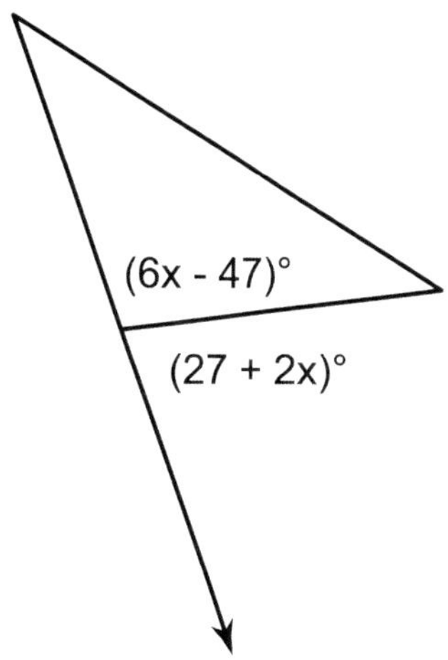

A) 45 B) 29

C) 25 D) 26

19) Find the value of x.

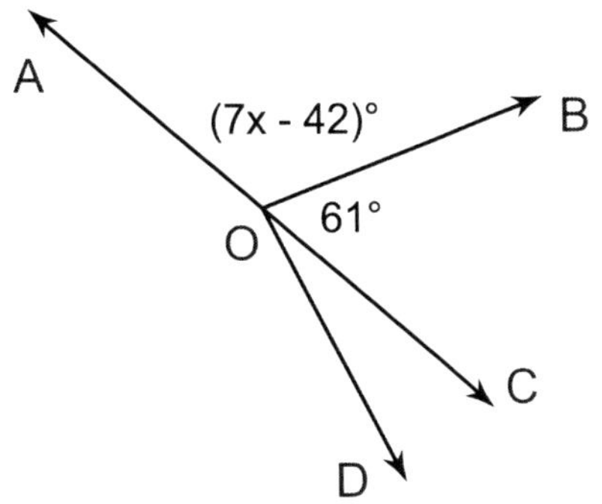

A) 23 B) 19

C) 20 D) 29

20) Find the value of x.

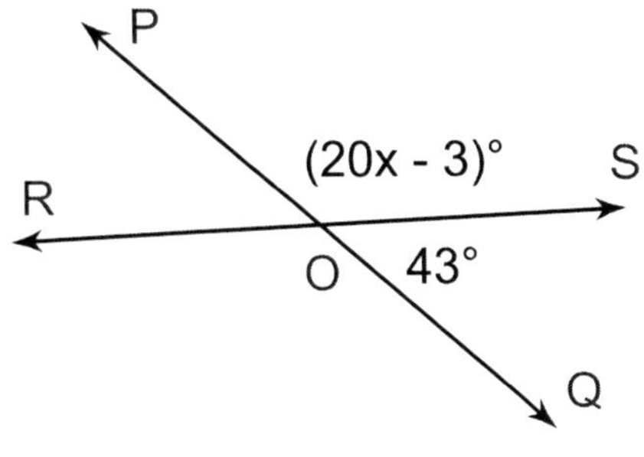

A) 7 B) 15

C) -3 D) 17

21) A rectangular prism measuring 9 km and 12 km along the base and 11 km tall

A) 1188 km^3 B) 2377.2 km^3

C) 2732.4 km^3 D) 1366.2 km^3

22) A rectangular prism measuring 14 yd and 9 yd along the base and 6 yd tall.

A) 861.8 yd^3 B) 357.7 yd^3

C) 756 yd^3 D) 715.3 yd^3

23) One lime costs \$0.30. How many limes can you buy for \$4.80?

24) If you can buy one cantaloupe for \$2.50, then how many can you buy with \$5?

25) 23 notebooks costs $20.70 for Nora. Find the unit rate of the note book.

26) 6 cookie boxes costs $15. Find the unit price of a cookie box.

27) A square prism measuring 13 km along each edge of the base and 11 km tall. Find the surface area.

A) 227.5 km² *B) 910 km²

C) 113.8 km² D) 455 km²

28) Find the distance between chantilly and Gainsville on a map with a scale of 1 cm : 18 km if they are actually 180 km apart.

29) Herndon and Bethesda are 3 cm apart on a map that has a scale of 1 cm : 19 km. How far apart are the real cities?

30) Find the distance between San Jose and San Ramon on a map with a scale of 1 in : 3 mi if they are actually 21 mi apart.

31) Mary was planning a trip to Bolivia. The exchange rate is $1 to 8 Bolos. How many Bolos would she get if he exchanged $1.80?

32) The money used in Toro town is called the Toros. The exchange rate is 8 Toros for every $1. Find how many dollars you would receive if you exchanged 18.4 Toros.

33) Nora took a trip to Argentina. Upon leaving she decided to convert all of her Pesos back into dollars. How many dollars did she receive if she exchanged 17.4 Pesos at a rate of $1 for every 3.1 Pesos?

34) Compare the data measures of the below data sets

Rainfall in July 2020

177	174	173	174	177	180
181	170	183	179	173	184
176	176	184	175	174	

Rainfall in August 2020

184	178	169	179	180	174
179	187	174	175	173	178
176	182	183	174	176	

(A) Mean value in rainfall july is greater than rainfall in august

(B) Median value of rainfall in July is more than in august

(C) Median value of rainfall in august is more than in july

(D) Median values remains same

35) Compare the data measures of the below data sets

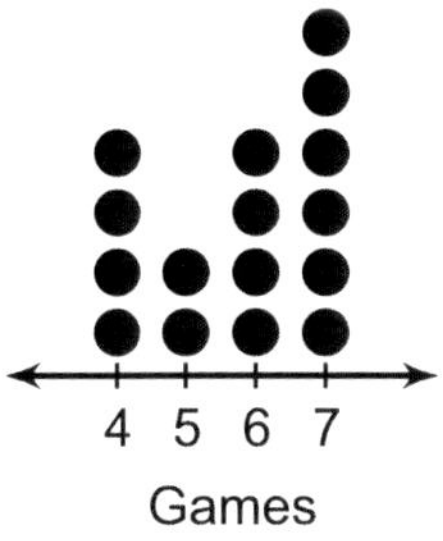

(A) Mode is greater than median

(B) Mean is greater than median

(C) Mode is less than mean

(D) Mean and median are same

36) Compare the data measures of the below data sets

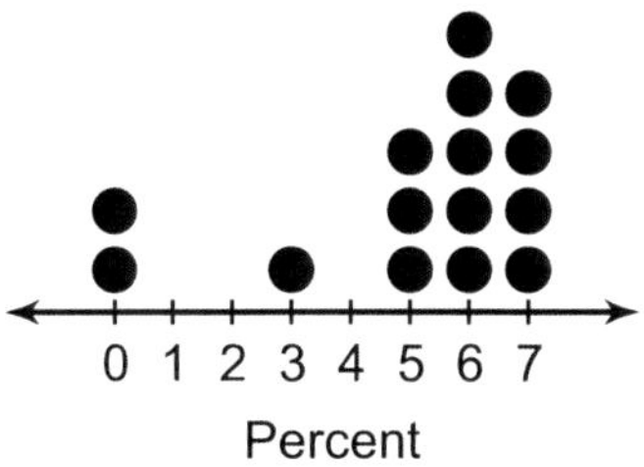

(A) Mode is greater than median

(B) Mean is greater than mode

(C) Mode is less than mean

(D) Mode and median are same

37) Area of square ABCD is 25 sq.ft. If the length of the side is increased three times, then the new area of square ABCD is

38) At the deadly turnof highway I701 every one car out of 7 cars met with an accident this month. If 1407 cars crossed this turn then what is the probability of number of cars who met with an accident?

39) Sam solves 4 out of 5 puzzles correctly. If he solves 505 puzzles how many did he solve correctly?

40) Which equation shows the relation between x and y?

x	y
10	29
12	27
19	20
5	34

(A) x - y = 39

(B) x + y = 39

(C) x + 12 = y

(D) x + 30 = 34

41) Which equation shows the relation between x and y?

x	y
1	3
3	9
4	12
5	15

(A) y = x + 3

(B) y = 4x

(C) y = x + 6

(D) y = 3x

42) Find the average of the data below

38 , 48 , 39 , 38 , 42

43) Find the area of the below

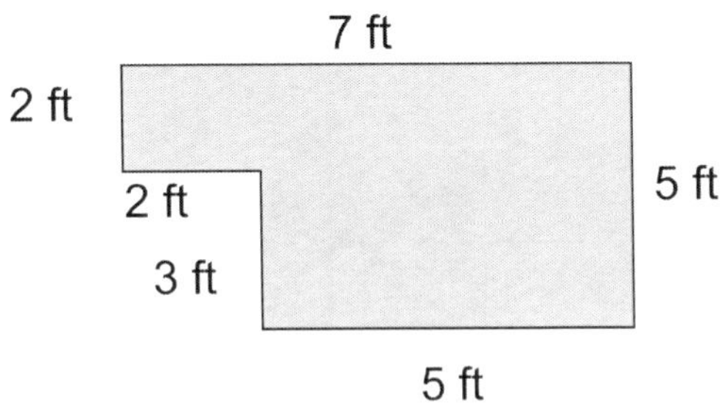

44) Mighty moses lab orders new cells with a diameter of 0.000055. Express this in scientific notation

(A) 0.55×10^{-5} (B) 55×10^{-8}

(C) 5.5×10^{-5} (D) 0.055×10^{-7}

45) Sam, the painter, paints 1 ft in 5 seconds. In half an hour, how much sq.ft of painting is completed?

(A) 360 sq.ft (B) 180 sq.ft

(C) 250 sq.ft (D) 150 sq.ft

46) Tasty bites restaurant has 3 appetizers, 2 rice dishes, 5 salads and 3 desserts available. In how many different ways can he or she choose one of each dish for lunch?

(A) 11 ways (B) 90 ways

(C) 18 ways (D) 29 ways

47) Moving lawn company charges $25 for every 80 sq.ft. How much does it cost to move if each lawn has an area of 260 sq.ft?

48) Sam eats exactly half cookies for breakfast from what he has left on previous day. On sunday evening he bought 80 cookies from the bakery. How many cookies are left after breakfast on Friday?

49) Kim knots 10 sweaters in 8 hours. At this rate, how many can she knit in 628 hours ?

50) Restaurant R offers a 10% discount on lunch buffet today. The lunch buffet was originally priced at $15. How much should Jolly and Molly should pay for lunch today?

(A) $ 3 (B) $ 25

(C) $ 27 (D) $ 33

51) Simplify the below

$(5 + 1)^2 + (5 \div 1) - (5^2 + 1^2)$

52) Simplify the below

$(121 \div 11)^2 + 6 \times 5 - 1$

53) Given a = 11, b = 12

Simplify 3 + a x 2 - b x 2

54) Which of the below sets has the highest value of range?

(A) {6,10,3,9,6} (B) {5,1,6,4,2}

(C) {6,9,7,4,5} (D) {7,4,3,4,5}

Grade 7
Answer Keys

Test 1		Test 1		Test 2		Test 2	
1.	C	30.	D	1.	A	30.	C
2.	C	31.	A	2.	D	31.	C
3.	D	32.	C	3.	B	32.	A
4.	D	33.	D	4.	C	33.	B
5.	D	34.	D	5.	D	34.	B
6.	B	35.	B	6.	C	35.	D
7.	A	36.	B	7.	D	36.	C
8.	B	37.	B	8.	B	37.	A
9.	D	38.	D	9.	A	38.	D
10.	D	39.	C	10.	D	39.	B
11.	C	40.	A	11.	C	40.	B
12.	A	41.	C	12.	B	41.	C
13.	A	42.	A	13.	D	42.	B
14.	B	43.	C	14.	A	43.	A
15.	A	44.	A	15.	C	44.	D
16.	C	45.	C	16.	A	45.	25
17.	A	46.	\$1.69	17.	C	46.	10
18.	B	47.	\$0.80	18.	C	47.	160 mi
19.	A	48.	\$1.19	19.	B	48.	\$4.81
20.	D	49.	190 mi	20.	A	49.	11.5 dirhums
21.	A	50.	C	21.	A	50.	D
22.	A	51.	A	22.	B	51.	B
23.	D	52.	$\frac{1}{84}$	23.	D	52.	$\frac{1}{8}$
24.	B	53.	224.5 sq.ft	24.	C	53.	72 sq.m
25.	A	54.	1.5 kg	25.	A	54.	\$143,500
26.	C	55.	$13x + 102 = 180$, $x = 6$	26.	B	55.	$12x + 156 = 180$, $x = 2$
27.	A			27.	A		
28.	B			28.	D		
29.	D			29.	C		

Test 3		Test 3	
1.	A	30.	C
2.	D	31.	D
3.	C	32.	A
4.	A	33.	D
5.	B	34.	A
6.	A	35.	A
7.	A	36.	D
8.	A	37.	D
9.	D	38.	C
10.	A	39.	D
11.	C	40.	D
12.	C	41.	B
13.	B	42.	C
14.	D	43.	C
15.	D	44.	D
16.	C	45.	A
17.	A	46.	D
18.	A	47.	A
19.	D	48.	B
20.	C	49.	28
21.	B	50.	140 mi
22.	D	51.	Mode = 50&51
23.	C		Median = 50
24.	A	52.	Mean = 9.13
25.	C		Median = 8
26.	D	53.	195 votes
27.	C	54.	4x + 112 = 180
28.	B		x = 17
29.	A	55.	D Median = 54

Test 4		Test 4	
1.	B	30.	30 miles
2.	D	31.	$3.69
3.	A	32.	14.7 kross
4.	D	33.	4 cm
5.	C	34.	10 in
6.	C	35.	C
7.	C	36.	D
8.	B	37.	6400 sq.ft
9.	A	38.	21
10.	D	39.	201 boxes
11.	A	40.	B
12.	D	41.	A
13.	B	42.	41 sq.cm
14.	A	43.	32
15.	D	44.	B
16.	C	45.	7 pairs
17.	C	46.	B
18.	A	47.	A
19.	A	48.	781.25 cells
20.	D	49.	C
21.	C	50.	A
22.	A	51.	57
23.	C	52.	64
24.	B	53.	35
25.	4	54.	D
26.	9	55.	8x + 192 = 360
27.	6		x = 21
28.	$0.69		
29.	$7.10		

Test 5		Test 5	
1.	C	30.	7 in
2.	A	31.	14.4 Bolos
3.	D	32.	$2.30
4.	B	33.	$5.61
5.	A	34.	C
6.	A	35.	A
7.	C	36.	D
8.	A	37.	225 sq.ft
9.	B	38.	201 cars
10.	A	39.	404
11.	A	40.	B
12.	C	41.	D
13.	D	42.	41
14.	B	43.	29 sq.ft
15.	D	44.	C
16.	B	45.	A
17.	D	46.	B
18.	C	47.	$152.50
19.	A	48.	2.5 cookies
20.	A	49.	81 sweaters
21.	A	50.	C
22.	C	51.	15
23.	16	52.	150
24.	2	53.	1
25.	$0.90	54.	A
26.	$2.50	55.	15x + 105 = 360
27.	B		x = 17
28.	10 cm		
29.	57 km		

Made in United States
North Haven, CT
15 July 2025

70721507R00041